THE MANAGER'S BOOK OF
DECENCIES

HOW SMALL GESTURES BUILD GREAT COMPANIES

STEVE HARRISON

McGraw-Hill

New York   Chicago   San Francisco   Lisbon
London   Madrid   Mexico City   Milan   New Delhi
San Juan   Seoul   Singapore   Sydney   Toronto

2 3 4 5 6 7 8 9 0   DOC/DOC   0 9 8 7

ISBN-13: 978-0-07-148633-0
ISBN-10: 0-07-148633-X

McGraw-Hill books are available at special quantity discounts to use as premiums and sales promotions, or for use in corporate training programs. For more information, please write to the Director of Special Sales, Professional Publishing, McGraw-Hill, Two Penn Plaza, New York, NY 10121-2298. Or contact your local bookstore.

This book is printed on acid-free paper.

*This book is dedicated to the memory of
my father, Albert P. Harrison, MD*

"Where there is no man, be one."

Contents

Part Three: Building the Decent Organization 151

Foreword

Corporate culture is the heartbeat and lifeblood of any corporation or organization. A company's culture is a critical element to its success. Offering simple common courtesies and showing respect to others generate not only loyalty but also a sense of self-purpose that pumps life into any organization.

This book's subtitle, *How Small Gestures Build Great Companies*, exemplifies how we have run our businesses over the last 40 years. Whether starting out with my first travel company in the early 1960s, The Los Angeles Olympic Organizing Committee, or being the commissioner of Major League Baseball, the common thread of organizations I have worked for is a positive business culture. How we treat one another, our customers, investors, vendors, and partners sustains any business or group.

When I think of the leaders in my life who have had the most impact on how I conduct business, I realize they all practiced small decencies at every opportunity. Kirk Kerkorian, a leader I admire in many ways, gave me my first break when I was 22 years old by hiring me to help him manage Trans International Airlines. Kerkorian is a master at the "two-minute schmooze" described in *The Manager's Book of Decencies*. This is the decency that recognizes that the most invisible people in the organization are as significant as anyone else. I never saw Kirk ignore a receptionist or accept a car key from a parking lot attendant without taking a minute to visit and to recognize the individual. When Kirk asks someone, "How are you doing?" he really does want to know. He is decent enough to actually listen to the answer.

Decencies are a habit that start early in life, and they should instinctively feel right to us. Here's an example of a small decency I recommend. On the day that an individual new to our organization starts work, we send flowers and a card to the new hire's spouse or partner. In the card we acknowledge that the individual has started a new journey with our firm and that we see that person's spouse or partner is important to our team as well.

This book covers dozens of ideas for small decencies. Especially important are those around the issue of terminating employees. Job loss, downsizing, and terminations are unfortunate realities of today's business environment. How we treat affected individuals and how we help preserve dignity and self-respect are critical to them as human beings.

In this book, it is evident that Steve Harrison is passionate about helping individuals redirect their lives when their work situations change. There are not enough people who focus on the needs of the individuals who are victims of restructuring and downsizing. Steve's business card may identify him as a founding principal of one of the world's largest outplacement firms, but he is really in the transfer-of-strength business. Steve and his colleagues know that a little coaching, a little training, and a new perspective can transform those negatives into positives that can lead to new engaging careers.

This book is not about business in the sense of the transfer of goods and services, but rather the business of people, the business of ethics, and the business of culture. The book describes corporate cultures that inspire a sense of purpose and empower human beings to do their best in any environment or business climate.

The concepts in this book can be helpful resources for developing that kind of culture in support of a business or organization. The ideas help meet the growing need for great organizations at every level.

Peter V. Ueberroth
Chairman, Contrarian Group
Newport Beach, California

Acknowledgments

All authors, even prolific ones, have a "first book" experience. Mine is now complete. *The Manager's Book of Decencies*, more than an experience, has been an unforgettable journey. If I've learned nothing else, I've learned that writing a book, like raising children, takes a village. In my case, this village is populated by many people who cared about, motivated, and inspired me. I'm grateful to all those whose unselfish decency helped pull me through the highs, the lows, and the ongoing challenge of connecting the dots when I saw too few connections and too many dots.

As always, this book could not have been written without the love and support of my family. Thanks go to my wife, Shirley, the love of my life, for her unwavering confidence. I appreciate our daughters, Amy and Leslie, and their spouses, Abs and Jonathan. Thanks go also to my son, Mark. And I don't want to leave out my grandchildren, Chloe and Jacob. You all have my deepest gratitude for all that we have shared together.

I am in debt to a number of people who got this book off on the right path. They include my book consultant, John Kador, who taught me the difference between writing and writing a book. I'm grateful to Katherine Armstrong, our content editor, who thankfully said, "Not so fast!" after we'd put our pens down.

At McGraw-Hill, I appreciate Mary Glenn, who believes in decency as a critical business success factor.

I also acknowledge Bob Lee, author, teacher, and founder of Lee Hecht Harrison, whose knowledge of leadership theory and corporate culture helped clear the path; and Orville Pierson, my LHH professional colleague, who insisted that I "just do it!"

I'm indebted to Lynn Erickson, my colleague and research and speech coordinator, for her resourcefulness.

Countless others have contributed decencies for this book or read the book in its several iterations. I'm thankful to Amy Lyman, co-founder of The Great Place to Work Institute, for her generous gift of time, enthusiasm, resources, and commitment to excellence in corporate culture. I appreciate Jim Kouzes, the well-known leadership author and consultant, for his counsel on the leadership imperative in corporate culture. My gratitude extends to Theresa Welbourne, CEO of eePulse, one of the country's prominent researchers and thought leaders on employee engagement and retention. A heartfelt thank you goes to ethicist Jim Lukaszewski and compliance attorney Joe Murphy, both smart and streetwise around the new ethics and compliance revolution; author and consultant David Noer, who has reminded so many of us of the price to be paid for not leading; and John Knapp, director of the Southern Institute for Business & Professional Ethics, for helping to demystify the complexities of ethics and corporate governance.

This book would not have been possible without the support of the leadership at Adecco and Lee Hecht Harrison who provided me with the time and resources to bring *The Manager's Book of Decencies* to fruition.

Steve Harrison

Introduction

I don't think I chose the topic for this book. I think it chose me.

I've been fortunate to know decency in multiple manifestations. My father was a psychiatrist, and my wife is a psychologist. Both have been dedicated to helping people live lives that they feel good about. As a child, I would watch my father greet medical interns at our home from my perch on the staircase. If caught on that staircase, I was quickly shooed away. That's how I learned about confidentiality and respect for the sanctity of the doctor-patient relationship. My father's job was to listen—perhaps the ultimate decency of all. Patients in various states of unwellness would be considered, and my father was there to help the interns think about all aspects of the care of the *total* patient.

My quarter century in the career management and outplacement industry—or, as I like to say, the "transfer of strength" business—has only served to magnify my understanding of the power of decencies.

Job loss, notorious as one of life's greatest stresses, can devastate even the strongest among us. Job loss can unravel the surest sense of confidence and the most stable of lives. I have seen this despair over job loss firsthand. In more ways than one, effective outplacement is a business of decency. Our role is not only to provide strength and career survival strategies, but also to create an enabling environment in which those in need can experience support, understanding, and professional decency at their lowest moments.

When I was asked in 2004 to accept the role as the first ever corporate compliance officer for our parent company, Adecco, I did so with initial reservations. I didn't want to resign from Lee Hecht Harrison, the company I had helped build and then merge with Swiss-based Adecco. I was initially overwhelmed by the learning curve of my new job. But it was one of the best decisions of my life. I not only helped create a vital and lasting function for the company, but I also met with hundreds of employees and helped clarify the issues for them.

I listened to their reactions, which evolved as much out of the post-Enron environment as their own experiences. I learned that most were somewhat aware of the Sarbanes-Oxley Act. But I discovered that company culture was always their priority. In one of these meetings, Lenny Agrillo, a longtime member of Adecco North America's building maintenance staff, was especially eloquent. He said, "Steve, this legal compliance stuff is flying over us at 30,000 feet. Don't the regulators understand that the real deal is at ground level where we all need to feel good about coming to work?"

Lenny's comment resonated particularly loudly when I realized that the regulators, especially the federal sentencing commissioners, had themselves learned some lessons from Enron and Sarbanes-Oxley. During the hearings they conducted in 2004, the commissioners learned that the heavy hand of the law had not produced the anticipated reduction in reported incidents of fraud and gross misconduct among public companies. They learned that there was a growing body of opinion that the silver bullet lay not only in strengthened new compliance laws, but also in strengthened corporate cultures. Regulators called for companies to "promote an organizational culture that encourages ethical conduct." But I have yet to see specifically what they meant by those words.

The new compliance laws did indeed affect companies, but probably not in the way their creators had in mind. Public corporations grappled with the high monetary costs and administrative burden of compliance. As regulations increased the onus on directors, companies found it difficult to fill empty board seats with qualified people willing to take the risk of being held to the emerging standards. Companies around the world question whether being listed on the public markets is worth the risk under these circumstances.

I can imagine Lenny saying, "You're looking in the wrong end of the telescope. The devil is in the details."

So let's take Lenny's advice and break out the magnifying glass.

This book is about the details. The details in this case consist of hundreds, maybe thousands, of small gestures of decency offered by individuals who have no expectation of reward. In this book, I present examples of decencies that have come from real employees and managers in real companies. These sometimes unsung heroes have introduced creative, natural, and decent gestures that serve to define ethical culture more precisely and actively.

For corporate management, decencies give meaning and texture to the ubiquitous values statements framed on office walls. To the regulators and governing authorities, decencies can offer a fast lane to the heretofore unanswered question, "What specifically does an ethical culture look like?" To Lenny and his counterparts around the world, decencies make the conversation about corporate ethics more palpable. For me, decencies are a way to make the often theoretical dialogue about leadership, integrity, and ethics less elusive and theoretical and more tangible and realistic.

It would be easy for us in the corporate community to hide behind the imprecision of the term *ethical culture* as if to wait for yet another trend to blow over. The greater opportunity is to seize the recognized importance of corporate culture and use it in service of our organizations. I am one executive who won't let the talk of ethical culture be a throwaway.

Given today's headlines, it is easy to be a pessimist about our work institutions. "If you keep saying that things are going to be bad, you have a good chance of becoming a prophet," Isaac Bashevis Singer observed. Perhaps, but I'm not interested in prophets that divine hopelessness. Without hope there can be no change. This is the time for a culture of decencies, optimism, and hope. As leaders, we must summon our will and mobilize all our resources to struggle against the forces of hopelessness and pessimism.

This book is just the beginning. It is intended to spark ideas, to incite momentum. I hope the book contributes to a conversation that accelerates the process of enriching work cultures. Your own examples of the decencies you've experienced in corporate life can be a force multiplier as together we try to make every company a reflection of our best instincts and highest aspirations. Reaching for the best we are capable of is the challenge facing us. Together, one decency at a time, we can build purposeful corporate cultures that harness our energies to benefit the rapidly shrinking world we share.

Part One
Small Changes, Big Results

Small decencies are individual gestures that help define the larger environment and thereby become the building blocks of an ethical culture. Regulatory approaches to making corporations more law-abiding and ethical were supposed to restore investor confidence through greater transparency, increased accountability, and improved governance. However, evidence shows that the unintended consequences are ham-fisted responses by companies reacting to heavy-handed regulations. All this reminds us of discredited management models of command and control. Regulations by themselves can't move the needle to create well-behaved companies. Effective leadership, supported by a culture of decencies, does. Part One provides a working definition of business decencies and the role of leadership in creating the ethical cultures that regulation alone cannot.

1

We're Businesspeople, but First We're People

*Be faithful in small things because it is in them
that your strength lies.*

MOTHER TERESA

This is a book about leadership in action. Small actions, to be specific. These gestures, or decencies, are available to you immediately. People at every level of the organization have access to an unlimited number of them. These decencies generally require neither permission nor a budget. What they do require is action.

I believe that a company's culture can be molded—and for the better—by the cumulative power of small actions. But at its heart, this book is about the way we as leaders choose to behave—the actions we embrace—every day, especially during the quiet moments when we think no one is looking. So to begin, let's start not with theory but with a story of a simple act of decency that caught me by surprise, changed the way I related to my colleagues, and shifted, however slightly, the culture of my company for the better.

That company is Lee Hecht Harrison, a New Jersey–based career management firm specializing primarily in outplacement, the process of helping organizations and their employees deal with the effects of job loss. A few years ago, with the company growing quickly, the time was right to appoint a new chief operating officer. I wanted Ray, a West Point graduate and an MBA who had recently retired from the U.S. Army with the rank of brigadier general, to get to know our company. So we scheduled a tour, starting with several branch offices in the Northeast. At midmorning, we arrived at our first stop and passed through the glass doors into the familiar reception area. As usual, Melissa, the receptionist, was on duty.

"How are you, Melissa?" I asked casually.

"Fine. And you, Steve?"

"Great. Have a good day."

"You too."

I then proceeded toward the interior offices. Suddenly I found myself being pulled back into the reception area.

"What's wrong?" I asked Ray.

Ray said nothing, but guided me back to the reception desk. Then I watched as Ray made an ally and a memory. The first thing Ray did was stick out his right hand, a gesture reinforced by his charismatic smile that generated enough electricity to power a small town, and said, "Good morning, Melissa, I'm Ray. It's so great to meet you!"

After introducing himself, Ray launched into a dialogue with Melissa. "How long have you been with us?" "How did you hear about us?" "What did you do before you joined our firm?" "What kind of dog is that in the picture?" "What do you think of this business we're in together?" But it wasn't only one-way questions. He asked if Melissa had questions, and he answered them candidly. Melissa was obviously delighted with the exchange.

"Well, nice to meet you," Ray said. "I look forward to seeing you next time I'm in." And as we went inside for our meeting, he said, "Keep doin' what you're doin', Melissa. We need you!"

As I closed the door to the meeting area, I looked at Ray. "What was that all about?" He answered: "It's called the *two-minute schmooze*. Our receptionists meet or talk by phone to more people critical to our company in one day than you or I will meet in the course of a year: people at all levels, from all of our branches everywhere, our customers, our suppliers, our colleagues, our bosses, our applicants and job-seekers. Melissa and the dozens like her are nothing less than our concierge desk. They control our reputation. And anyway, it's a decent thing to do. Just the decent thing to do."

The decent thing to do. Of course I had heard the words before, but I hadn't put them in the context of how we act at work. Ray's two-minute schmooze is how I first learned of the power of small decencies, and it's a perfect illustration of decent leadership and the impact it has on organizations. "Organizations have a feel about them," says Charles Handy in *The Hungry Spirit*. Small decencies release that feel, "a feel which the visitor picks up as soon as he or she enters the building or, often merely encounters one of the people who work there."

THE POWER OF DECENCY

Even though treating others with humanity and respect is timeless, John Cowan may have been the first to bring the concept explicitly into the workplace. In his book *Small Decencies*, Cowan writes:

As I come in the door of a business for the first time, I automatically check for the telltales. Is there a place for the visitor's coat? Am I offered a cup of coffee? Am I an interruption to the receptionist or a welcome guest? Am I to wait for my appointment, or does the person who called me in arrive immediately and with enthusiasm at my appearance? Is the phone put on hold? Is there time to talk? A place on the table for my notebook? Adjustments made for my well-being?

These things are inconsequential by themselves . . . But as an indicator of the spirit of the person I am meeting, or the culture of the business I am dealing with, these small decencies are excellent telltales. Their absence screams of personal disrespect, harried and overworked people, a harsh or cold atmosphere, an environment corrosive to the human spirit. Their presence almost infallibly suggests attention to the needs of people beyond the need for a cup of hot coffee.

How to create and sustain an ethical and compliant culture through the deployment of decencies is the main concern of this book. The common thread is that ethical behavior is almost the inadvertent side effect of focusing on something else in addition to generating results. Let's focus, instead, on small business decencies for their own sake precisely because doing so brings meaning to the workplace. If we do that, if we offer decencies for their own sake without expecting a specific outcome, I believe that the corporate cultures in which we operate will grow in the ways we desire.

The acid test Cowan suggests, is this: "Think of your children or cherished loved ones. Would you want your son or daughter to live in your corporation? To be shaped by it? Small decencies remind us that we can be true to our values both at home and at work, and that the more humanely we treat one another, the better we will be as people, and the better we will be in doing our life's work." All this is by way of saying that we are businesspeople, but first we're people. We are colleagues who can make a difference in another person's day, and we're people who want to be treated with respect, humanity, and caring. Out of such actions, multiplied dozens of times a day over a period of time, corporate cultures take root and sprout a thousand points of light.

Ted Koppel, one of the great journalists of our time, underscored the importance of small decencies in the power of individuals to make a difference. Speaking to the graduates of Stanford University in 1998, he referred to the "small acts of courage and kindness" that are required to challenge practices and institutions that limit human possibilities:

> We will not change what's wrong with our culture through legislation, or by choosing up sides on the basis of personal popularity or party affiliation. We will change it by small acts of courage and kindness; by recognizing, each of us, his or her own obligation to set a proper example.
>
> Aspire to decency. Practice civility toward one another. Admire and emulate ethical behavior wherever you find it. Apply a rigid standard of morality to your lives; and if, periodically, you fail as you surely will, adjust your lives, not the standards.
>
> There's no mystery here. You know what to do. Now, go out and do it!

At the end, Koppel underscores the action aspect of decencies. Decencies have no value until we act them out. But we know from our own experience that acting upon a decision is difficult, especially when we have reason to believe we may be criticized for taking a stand. So we may be excused for reframing Koppel's final imperative into a question: "Now, will you go out and do it?"

In other words, do we have the fortitude to act on our values? There is no easy answer to this question—but it must be repeatedly asked. Some leaders avoid this question only at the great cost of distancing themselves from those they serve. Leaders will make mistakes, but in testing themselves—with each slip and each recovery—they will find the strength they need to prevail. Finding this out is not for the faint of heart, but then again, neither is being a leader.

DEFINING DECENCY

All of us, at one time or another, have used the word *decency* or its variants. We may associate decency with being considerate, courteous, gracious, honest, honorable, thoughtful, appropriate, tasteful, respectable, obliging, or helpful. We talk of decent acts, decent behaviors, a decent person, a decent wage. We find ourselves relating to a word that reflects specific behaviors. Even the opposite, *indecent*, is something that most of us can relate to: "indecent exposure" is quite vivid to us. "Are you decent?" was originally backstage theater jargon for "Are you dressed?"

Here's a typical dictionary definition of decencies:

Gestures, surroundings, or services deemed necessary for an acceptable standard of living.

I'd like to extend the definition for our purposes:

A business decency is a gesture freely offered without expectation of reward that, in ways small and large, changes the corporate culture for the better.

This definition may be a bit obscure, so let me unpack it a little.

A decency is a discrete *gesture* or *action*. It's verblike in that a decency must be acted out for it to have meaning. It's not an intention or attitude, although both of these often come first. Wanting to be decent is like wanting to lose weight. "I want to be decent" has as much to do with actually being decent as "I want to lose weight" has to do with actually losing weight. Intentions are good, but actually being decent, like actually losing weight, requires action.

A genuine decency is *freely offered*. A decency cannot be compelled by a supervisor or required by a policy. It is voluntary on the part of the individual offering it because, in this instance, it is consistent with the individual's—and, hopefully, the organization's—values. Please don't confuse decencies with obligations or mandates. Offering employees safe working conditions is not, by the definition of this book, a decency; it's just the minimum requirement for being in business codified by such bodies as the U.S. Occupational Safety and Health Administration (OSHA). An equal opportunity workplace free of harassment is not a decency; it's an expectation that has become the norm and is enforced by the rule of law. While the continuum between decencies and mandates is always evolving, what's important is that at the time the small decency gesture is made, the giver is acting of his or her own volition.

Without expectation of reward is critical. If you offer a gesture with the expectation of explicit reciprocity, it becomes a form of barter. There is nothing wrong with this; the vast bulk of human interactions operate on this basis. I'll help you cut your lawn if you help me build my fence. A gesture, however decent, offered to advance an explicit motive, however beneficial, is not a decency, but a bribe. Having an ulterior or hidden motive also negates the decency. People can usually smell a hidden agenda coming a mile away, and when they do, they run, not walk, the other way.

True decencies are not transactional. It's the unilateral and spontaneous quality of decencies that make them so unexpected and powerful. For that reason, decencies are no longer merely transactional; they are transformational. They have the power to transform both the giver and the receiver and affect the culture at the same time.

There is, I admit, a bit of a contradiction here. I argue that deciding to offer small decencies is a way to change corporate culture, which is of inestimable value. But I also say that a decency is offered without expectation of reward or specific outcome. Which is it? I reconcile the matter this way: the decision to offer a decency does, indeed, produce a benefit (a positive change in the culture). We have no way of knowing what that benefit is or when it will be redeemed. While we certainly expect our organizations to benefit, we expect no *personal* benefit. On that basis, I claim that decencies are offered without any expectation of reward. There can be no ROI analysis of a decency precisely because it cannot be measured, and in the effort to apply a metric, it ceases being a decency.

There is in the decision to act with decency the hope that we will change the culture for the better. Is this hopeful link between culture change and decencies itself an ulterior motive? Perhaps, but that's okay. The decision to act with decency is part of the responsibility of leadership: it is up to each of us to steer the cultures in which we work. What is not okay, what does *not* work, is when a decency is offered with the specific expectation of a *quid pro quo* from the receiver. In the two-minute schmooze example, Ray knew he was investing in our "concierge desk" because it was good for business. That's doing the right thing for our organization. What's important is that he wasn't looking for Melissa to do something specifically for him, such as changing travel arrangements or getting him a cup of coffee.

In the corporate setting, I argue that decency has a vital place. John Cowan's vivid description of what he thinks about when approaching a reception desk is eloquent in its symbolism. The importance of acts of decency in the organizational context cannot be underestimated. They need to satisfy important criteria in order to be unambiguously reflective of cultural health.

More than the leadership philosophy that is manifested by the CEO, COO, or others in the "C-suite," decencies form the package of messages that the organization delivers to its members. The unifying theme of these messages rounds out a set of norms that clearly define the limits between acceptable and unacceptable behavior. The messages help the participants act genuinely as members of a community. The messages are so ingrained that they give the members of the community confidence to assert "That's not how we do things around here" when faced with a violation of the culture.

Decency messages signal many things. "Warm and fuzzy" is one of them, and that's okay. But there's an element of rigor to decencies, especially if we want them to be effective on a large scale. Based on my research, effective decencies have many of the following characteristics:

- *Actionable.* A decency is both an action and a catalyst for action. The only effective way for an organization to change is by changing behavior. The act of choosing to perform a decency signals an immediate change in the behavior of the manager who offers it. The behavior of the person who receives the decency may also change. He or she may be inspired by the decency to perform better or communicate more effectively, or he or she may emulate the decency to other coworkers. Taken together, the initial action and the catalyzed action improve the culture of the organization for the better. Ray's two-minute schmooze was a discreet action—a conversation—that was a catalyst to encourage other managers to perform the same behavior.

- *Tangible.* A decency is capable of being handled or touched, or it causes a measurable change to the environment. An intangible decency, by contrast, is a virtue such as integrity or honesty. These are desirable qualities to strive for. When these qualities are expressed in a way that is tangible, then virtues become decencies. It is perceptible by the senses and memorable. Melissa, the receptionist, still recalls the specifics of her conversation with Ray many years later.

- *Practical.* A business decency must be guided by a sensibility that refers to good judgment, discrimination, and balance. It's not hard to let one's imagination run wild in a world of no constraints, but in business where constraints are very real, decencies that are pragmatic have the best opportunities for success. If the telephone had been ringing or other guests were waiting to be greeted, for instance, it wouldn't have been practical for Ray to engage Melissa for such an extended conversation.

- *Affordable.* A business decency must be within the financial means of the manager or organization. Small decencies, by definition, incur no or very little monetary cost. Ray's two-minute schmooze didn't cost a cent. Small decencies must also be affordable in other ways. They cannot encumber the organization with undue overhead, legal liability, or costly precedents.

- *Replicable.* Decencies must be replicable. Repeating the two-minute schmooze just strengthens its power. A decency offered to an individual is always welcome, but if the gesture is so constituted that it can be offered to *only* one individual, it does not rise to the level of a small decency. It's a one-off. A small decency should be able to function gracefully for more than one individual, in organizations of various sizes. Or it should be able to evolve within a single organization as the size of that organization expands or contracts.

- *Sustainable.* Decencies are best when they are implemented for today but are also available for the future. A decency is sustainable when the goodwill it generates for the organization over the long run more than compensates for the resources invested in it.

RIPPLES IN A POND:
THE IMPACT OF SMALL DECENCIES

I'd like to think I've mastered the two-minute schmooze, and I recommend it wholeheartedly. I've made friends with a lot of receptionists and listened to their stories. The two-minute schmooze subsequently became widely practiced throughout the company, as I discovered some years later.

I was visiting another branch office, many miles and many years remote from the place I first encountered the two-minute schmooze. By this time, the decency came naturally to me. As Nancy, the receptionist, and I were talking, Gary, the regional vice president asked Nancy to give me one of her business cards. Business cards for receptionists? That was new to me. Of course, I expressed immediate interest, and she proudly put a card in my hand. Under Nancy's name, her title stood out: "Director of First Impressions." I could only smile.

Like ripples in a pond, Ray's act at the reception desk sent a potent and positive message to Melissa, to the people sitting in the waiting area, to me, and eventually, to the organization. Without saying it, Ray made it clear that unhurried time with a colleague at any level was important; that the whole person, not just the job assignment was important; and that there was no room for executive pomposity in his demeanor. Ray started a buzz that found its way to other branch offices in the company. The title on the business card of the receptionist said it all. If you have any doubt as to the impact of the title, try this when you approach a reception desk anywhere: after identifying yourself, simply say, "So, you must be the director of first impressions." You'll have delivered a lasting dose of pride and self-worth.

That's the soft part of the decency's impact. Is there also a business impact? To me, the answer is a clear yes. Receptionists are for your company the concierge at the Ritz-Carlton; the first people your visitors meet; the traffic manager of relationships; the true differentiators of your brand. They have to be familiar with your business: not just your products, but your culture. Elevating them to "directors of first impressions" will create a band of ambassadors at the front doors of your business.

The two-minute schmooze costs nothing but pays off handsomely. It needs no one's permission to put into action and is replicable. The decency can be applied to organizations with one receptionist or hundreds. If the two-minute schmooze empowered just one receptionist, that fact would be enough justification for it. But the decency created ripples that spread to other locations, enriching the lives of an unknown number of people who work for the same company without necessarily knowing one another. Is it an impact that shows up on a balance sheet? Perhaps not. But perhaps the impact is more significant in that it shows up every time a receptionist—excuse me, *director of first impressions*—greets a visitor, answers the telephone, or responds to a question.

DECENCIES AT WORK

Organizations can learn from the example of New York City and other municipalities which subscribed to the "broken windows" theory of crime control, which says that property upkeep combined with the reduction of petty crimes such as graffiti enhance the livability of a place and reduce the incidence of more violent crimes. The broken-windows theory argues that crime is the inevitable result of disorder.

A window gets broken at an apartment building, but no one fixes it. It's left broken. Then something else gets broken. Maybe it's an accident, maybe not, but it isn't fixed either. Graffiti starts to appear. More and more damage accumulates. People walking by will conclude that no one cares and that no one is in charge. Soon, more windows will be broken, and the sense of anarchy will spread from the building to the street the window faces, sending a signal that anything goes. The whole neighborhood decays. Tenants move out. Crime moves in. The game is lost.

You don't believe it? Maybe it's a coincidence. Maybe there are good people and bad people in this world, and the things they do aren't dependent on their local environment. There's some very interesting social science research designed to test the theory that property upkeep is a factor in crime. Researchers in New York City went to one of the most blighted neighborhoods in the South Bronx. They took a nice, well-kept Jaguar automobile and parked it on the street. Then they retreated to a nearby apartment from where they could secretly see what attention the car attracted. Nothing happened. The car was parked for four days without anyone disturbing it. The researchers then made a slight adjustment to the experimental conditions.

They shattered one of the small windows on the passenger side of the car. That's all, a small broken window. Then they went back to their hidden viewing area. The result was startling. Within minutes people began inspecting the car. The first thing stolen was the radio. Four hours later, the car was stripped of its tires and all other valuables, turned upside down, and torched.

Malcolm Gladwell wrote about the broken-windows theory in his bestselling book, *The Tipping Point*. This is how he described it: "Consider a building with a few broken windows. If the windows are not repaired, the tendency is for vandals to break a few more windows. Eventually, they may even break into the building, and if it's unoccupied, perhaps become squatters or light fires inside. Or consider a sidewalk. Some litter accumulates. Soon, more litter accumulates. Eventually, people even start leaving bags of trash from take-out restaurants there or breaking into cars."

By the same token, an organization that ignores the value of small courtesies—making visitors welcome, insisting on clean restrooms, fixing peeling paint—signals that it is not likely to make customer or employee satisfaction a prime concern. A business that ignores small decencies is not likely to make business ethics a prime concern. What are the signs of a business that ignores small decencies? On one level, it tolerates the broken-windows symptoms of cynicism: winking at petty thefts of office supplies, cheating on expense reports, abuse of flextime and vacation policies. But more significantly, look for companies with employees who justify mistreating their customers because they are mistreated as employees.

A culture of ethics in business sustains itself with a constant focus on the details of small decencies. One can get a strong indication about how a company conducts itself and how it will attend to major ethical concerns by how it attends to seemingly minor ones. The reality, of course, is that it is in the small things that individuals or organizations reveal themselves.

In this way, a culture of decencies is really a sustained attitude across temptations big and small. Most of us recognize that if we are treated well, we tend to reciprocate in kind. By the same token, if we are mistrusted or disrespected, we tend to be mistrustful and disrespectful. In a real sense, what we see is what we get, or as Gandhi put it, we must be the change we want to bring about.

That's the disarming thing about decencies. While decencies can start with a leader's gesture, they really can't be imposed from the top down or implemented in a big strategic program.

Decencies must be modeled. They have to start small; offered one at a time on an individual level.

The challenges of running a business that operates both profitably and ethically confront us daily. It's difficult enough to do one or the other; delivering both eludes all but the most inspired leaders. We have but to consult today's headlines to realize how short of the ideal some organizations and executives continue to operate. The costs of failure are borne by all of us.

Many court cases, laws, regulations, board resolutions, whistle-blower hotlines, and codes of conduct later, the results are not encouraging. For all the talk about the crisis in public confidence and the "trust deficit," nurturing a culture of corporate citizenship is proving painfully difficult. Regulation, legislation, and a culture of punitive consequences are understandable reactions. But the reactions point to only a partial understanding of the problem. As we'll see in more detail in Chapter 2, punitive measures alone have not and will not change a culture. There is a better way to encourage corporate citizenship.

A critical source of competitive advantage is an organization's ability to create, manage, and leverage the many decencies it can bring to bear on the daily workings of the organization.

We all want the organizations and institutions we depend on to be well behaved, ethical, and compliant. We want to work in organizations that aspire to and achieve high levels of integrity. We want the values we hold important to be embodied in the daily behavior of our organizations, not just enshrined in codes of conduct and ethics statements. We want, quite simply, to be treated as human beings.

Every decency or lack of it advances or dilutes the existing culture of the organization. The stories that an organization tells about itself are critical. Decencies give the organization important clues about what its values are and how committed it is to their expression. If an organization seems uncaring, a solitary act of decency is not going to change the culture. But it may call some attention to the uncaring character of the organization in a powerful way. What's called for? More acts of decency until they are no longer solitary and no longer disarming.

DECENT LEADERSHIP

Decent leadership is a double entendre. In one sense, the words refer to leaders who do a decent *job* of what they're supposed to do: give direction to other people and their organization. But the phrase also refers to leading decently—leading people in a humane and respectful way.

It is the second meaning of the phrase that is the theme of this book. There is significant evidence and logic that this is the way to go for the future. It is a source of hope for all of us—the leaders, the led, and society generally.

The bottom line is that decencies are actions. You can't talk your way out of a situation that you behaved yourself into. This may be the ultimate test all corporate leaders should ask themselves: "If employees can look over my shoulder and see all my decisions, would they see me modeling the behaviors I want them to replicate?"

Conventional organizational wisdom makes several arguments against business decencies as I have defined them. The prevailing view flows from the assumption that all business behavior is basically driven by self-interest. The pay scales of CEOs and the general culture of self-entitlement that we live in certainly seem to affirm this assumption. This slice of conventional wisdom insists that for me to care about anything, there must be a payoff for me. Part Three of this book suggests that the payoff is indeed possible and that it's bigger than a return on self-interest. Deciding to offer true decencies is a choice we make regardless of what we are offered in return.

Part Two of this book lists many of these decencies in a form that readers can quickly and easily embrace. Most of these decencies cost little or nothing. Few require permission from anyone else. All represent small changes that can produce big results. Best of all, these decencies combine to create a corporate culture that helps protect the organization from acts of misconduct such as ethical lapses, workplace abuse, and fraud. These decencies are not dependent on individual CEOs (and that's good because the average turnover of CEOs is less than seven years). For that reason, decencies must not be dependent on specific leadership styles.

But what if, despite your best efforts at promoting a culture of decencies, the SEC investigates your company anyway? Then maybe you can take some comfort from this: the regulators may consider a pattern of decencies as mitigating evidence, and, perhaps, even as constructive intent to promote an ethical culture. A culture of decencies may not inoculate your organizations against every ethical transgression, but it may help minimize penalties.

There are no guarantees. However, decencies will improve the experience of work and, therefore, the culture of work.

2

A Funny Thing Happened on the Way to Compliance

Can capitalism be made more decent and its instrument,
business, work more obviously for the good of all, everywhere?

CHARLES HANDY, *THE HUNGRY SPIRIT*

I was in a pretty good place in early 2004. At an age when most executives are thinking of retiring, I was still enthusiastic about coming to work and facing new challenges. For 20 years or more, I had been operating at the senior levels of corporate life, running one of the world's largest outplacement/career management firms, Lee Hecht Harrison. My name was part of the business, and I was proud of what my partners and colleagues had achieved. We had started the firm in 1974 and turned it into a major player in the career management industry. In 1988, the firm was acquired by Swiss-based Adecco, the world's largest staffing company. Adecco saw Lee Hecht Harrison as a way to extend its brand beyond temporary staffing to offer on a worldwide basis a broader range of human capital solutions.

Let me digress a moment and define outplacement, because many people don't know what it is. This is what we say about it on our Web site:

Outplacement is the structured process of helping separated individuals evaluate their career opportunities, implement a job search and manage the transition to new employment, while receiving personal support and job search productivity tools.

In other words, *outplacement* is a process that combines professional coaching, practical guidance, and essential facilities to help terminated people at all levels move to the next stage in their careers. Organizations provide this support following individual or large-scale corporate change because it's good business, and when good people are laid off through no fault of their own, it is the decent thing to do. Individuals seek out outplacement or career management assistance when they need help to structure their job search, have been out of the job market for some time, or want to consider a new career direction.

As a result of the acquisition of our company by Adecco, I lived an engaging global experience. Adecco is a global, publicly traded company with a mostly European board of directors. After it acquired my firm, I became a member of Adecco's executive management committee. While I was based for most of the time at Lee Hecht Harrison's offices in northern New Jersey, I eventually had an office in Zurich too. Life was good. As an added bonus, I was observing America through the eyes of Europeans, an invaluable perspective that is one of the true benefits of globalization.

My frequent presence in the offices of the CEO and board of directors, and my tenure as part of the Adecco Group executive team, made it logical for Adecco to assign me to the role of interim chief compliance officer. In early 2004, I accepted that assignment and started working.

The deliverables of a compliance program are mandated by law. So I knew what to build. The law required publicly traded companies to have, among other things, a formal code of conduct, compliance training, a confidential "whistle-blower hotline," commitment to strict audits, certain adjustments to the ways boards of directors operate, certifications of the accounts from the CEO and finance managers, and comprehensive monitoring and documentation procedures. It was going to be expensive. I put a program outline together and presented it to a board composed mostly of European business leaders.

A number of other publicly traded companies had compliance programs in place, so I had some models. I made visits to trusted experts and advisors, made endless phone calls, and reviewed numerous documents. I set up appointments with consultants. We started a process that ultimately led to a code of conduct I am proud of. We refined the Adecco values statement. Finally a fledgling global compliance function was in place. A board resolution was signed. Today, Adecco makes compliance training available in print and online in multiple languages. The global confidential hotline was expanded and eventually outsourced. Internal controls were aligned following Sarbanes-Oxley requirements. Adecco people from senior executives to branch managers to rank-and-file employees then understood what was expected of them.

A year later, I handed the compliance responsibilities to my successor. I was named chairman of Lee Hecht Harrison and went back to New Jersey to help lead the outplacement company I loved.

But if I thought that all this compliance responsibility was out-of-sight/out-of-mind, I was wrong. True distance from my brief immersion in corporate compliance and ethics became impossible for me. For through this immersion, I became passionate not only about the hard-and-fast details of compliance, but about the more abstract and personal model of how corporate cultures are built and changed.

THE BIG STICK ALONE DOESN'T WORK

The key theme of the book is that compliance law is only part of the solution. My experience learning about Sarbanes-Oxley and other regulatory interventions has taught me that we can't create compliant organizations solely by punitive means. Carrots and sticks—heavy on the sticks—won't work without an organizational commitment to an ethical culture, as soft as that may sound. The building blocks of this kind of culture are decencies expressed in a variety of ways up and down the hierarchy.

When we lead people and our organizations to do the right things on a day-to-day basis, we become part of the solution, not the problem. In the beginning of the twenty-first century we seem to have a new problem—many of the leaders of our business organizations, the very people who are supposed to be solving problems, are in fact creating more of them. It isn't a brand-new issue, of course, but it seems to have taken on greater size as we enter the twenty-first century. The business journals are replete with stories about greed, failures in judgment, ethical violations, and a nonstop list of other sins—committed by the very people who should be setting the tone not only for our commercial enterprises, but for our larger society.

Corporate behavior matters more than it once did. Perhaps we see the recent examples of misbehavior in greater clarity, not just because of the larger numbers but also because our society's standards have been moving up. American business isn't just a private matter; whether or not businesses succeed has immense implications for the world economy we all share. We have come to expect more from leaders, and we are understandably distressed when they turn out to be scoundrels. To be sure, the shockers at Enron, WorldCom, Global Crossing, Tyco, Parmelat, Ahold, and too many others required a response. What was at stake was nothing less than confidence in the capital markets.

In the crisis atmosphere that followed the exposures of Enron and other companies, U.S. Senator Paul Sarbanes (a Democrat from Maryland) and Congressman Michael Oxley (a Republican from Ohio) rushed a comprehensive corporate compliance bill through Congress. The U.S. Securities and Exchange Commission (SEC), tasked with enforcing the bill, drafted a host of new regulations. The result? One really big stick and the formation of an ethics and compliance industry, of which I found myself an inextricable part.

Over the next few years, corporations all over the world incurred billions of dollars in compliance costs to meet the requirements imposed on all businesses participating in U.S. equity markets such as the New York Stock Exchange. Adecco, though based in Zurich, was expected to understand and comply with regulations emerging from Washington, DC. As a company whose shares are traded in the United States, Adecco and hundreds of other global companies were obliged to conform to new compliance policies. Suddenly it seemed that every public company was recruiting compliance/ethics officers. Even privately held firms paid attention, since many such firms want to preserve their ability to go public or be acquired by a public firm.

These companies understand that their operations must be in substantial compliance in order to preserve this option. As a result, people toiling in the backwaters of the corporate ethics and compliance function suddenly found themselves center stage in the new compliance industry.

With auditing firms, the bar was raised and earnings restatements became more frequent. News headlines were filled with reports of penalties. The SEC was taking names! Business magazines ran stories about impending corporate obituaries involving companies deemed too rigid to make the transition to the new environment of transparency and accountability. Virtually every major company that hadn't done so struggled to create and implement ethics codes and values statements.

But it became obvious that for all the evidence of crisis in public confidence, creating a business environment of compliance and corporate citizenship had proven painfully difficult. Regulation, legislation, and an atmosphere of punitive consequences were understandable reactions. Both regulators and the regulated focused on penalties: how to apply them and how to avoid them.

Unfortunately, early regulations reflected an incomplete understanding of the problem. Punitive measures alone had not and would not deliver the desired results. Regulatory responses such as Sarbanes-Oxley (SOX) were not enough; leadership programs were not enough; online ethics training was not enough; whistle-blower hotlines were not enough; board resolutions were not enough.

THE BIG "AHA!"—REGULATORS SEE THE LIGHT

Comforted by the enactment of Sarbanes-Oxley in mid-2002, and with three full years for publicly traded companies to comply fully, regulators may have hoped that the nightmare of executive misbehavior and financial and ethical shockers would soon come to an end, legislated to extinction. No such luck! Here's what they saw instead:

- In a November 2005 National Business Ethics Survey, 52 percent of respondents witnessed ethical misconduct. Only half of that number reported it to management.
- In another 2005 survey, it was found that while "for-profit companies have invested significant resources in ethics and compliance programs, we are not seeing much change in the direct impact these programs are having."
- A PricewaterhouseCoopers 2005 survey determined that, "The number of companies around the world that reported incidents of fraud increased 22 percent in the [previous] two years. 43 percent of surveyed people admitted to having engaged in at least one unethical act in the prior year."

What was happening? What went wrong? The situation had to evolve past the black and white of checklists. Regulators in the United States realized that the public interest would be better served if they worked to deter wrongdoing in the first place. But what would deter wrongdoing? The answer came to them, ironically, when discussing penalties.

The Federal Sentencing Commission, which was created in 1991 to provide guidelines to judges in exacting penalties for individual and corporate misconduct, held hearings in 2004 to evaluate their relevance in the post-Enron environment. What the commissioners heard during these sessions jolted them awake. "The goal of such programs is to not only comply with the law, but to instill in the organization's members an atmosphere of trust, a sense of mutual respect and benefit, and a commitment to doing the right thing, not simply the required thing," testified Dov Seidman, CEO of LRN, the world's largest online compliance training company. "I believe the Commission would have greater impact on organization behavior if it added the requirement that organizations promote an internal culture that encourages a commitment to both the law, as it has in the past, and to ethics." In further testimony, Seidman continued:

> Leadership is about values, not law. Is legal self-governance ("compliance") possible without a commitment to ethical self-governance? That is, will a focus on legal compliance alone be sufficient? We think not, because rules-based systems have tended to invite behavior that seeks to subvert the spirit of those rules while honoring their letter. Culture grounded in values and ethics has more sustainable success in establishing and maintaining higher standards of conduct than a culture that merely "encourages compliance."

Former SEC Commissioner Cynthia Glassman echoed this proposition by noting that, "Although the SEC can implement rules to incent good behavior, and enforce rules to disincent bad behavior, the agency cannot legislate ethical behavior." So the stage was now set for a new government perspective. Was the heavy hand of compliance law ready to morph into a kinder and gentler strategy? Language introduced in the revised sentencing guidelines issued in November 2004 stated that public companies must do two things:

- Promote an organizational culture that encourages ethical conduct and commitment to compliance with the law.
- Ensure that their standards are promoted through "appropriate incentives to perform in accordance with the compliance and ethics program."

This was the regulators' new bullet. This language could mean that if two organizations were guilty of the same wrongdoing and Company A was deemed to promote an ethical culture and Company B was not, then Company A could expect a mitigated penalty. In other words, regulators might well impose a lower fine. This was a significant development, as fines and penalties are substantial. Predictably, companies clamored to understand just what constituted promoting an ethical culture.

In this quest companies were stymied. The Ethics & Compliance Officer Association held conferences in 2005 and 2006 with an eye toward answering the critical question: "What does an ethical culture look like?" The answers provided by the panelists at these conferences were circular at best. Ethical corporate cultures, in the eyes of the regulators, were characterized by:

- An effective code of conduct (but we knew that—it's the law)
- A compliance officer or someone in charge (the law)
- A confidential whistle-blower hotline (the law)
- Compliance training (the law)
- Incentives for compliance and ethical conduct (revised sentencing guidelines)

- Communication and commitment
- Ethics "performance" covered in employee evaluations and bonus calculations
- Ethics incorporated into job descriptions, competencies, and integrating employees into the work environment

If an ethical culture is nothing more than a restatement of the law, plus an array of programs, policies, and procedures, it begs the question. It's like defining a word by referencing it to itself. However, when we look to the creators of the revised sentencing guidelines for clarification of the meaning of the phrase "ethical culture," we come away thirsting for more.

To be fair, ethical culture is difficult to define. Many companies still struggle with what it means. Understandably, some leaders avoid grappling with such a complicated issue and set it aside for another day. But I am not content that regulators are making ethical culture a footnote in business history. Throughout this book, I attempt to wrestle with the idea of ethical culture in terms that are not just a restatement of regulation. Of course programs and policies are important. But an ethical culture requires more. What it requires is a foundation of attitudes and decencies. These decencies make up the building blocks of the ethical culture. They are low cost, easy to use, and universally applicable.

Beating on the compliance drum is not the only way to create the kind of corporate cultures that predict good citizenship. Laws, by themselves, are inadequate to the task. Programs based on leadership training and consulting, by themselves, don't do it. What does? How do you soften the underbelly of the corporate giant, armored and often resistant to change, so that it is ready for compliance?

My answer is swift: by fertilizing the ground of corporate cultures with decencies so that legal compliance initiatives can more easily take root. We have to create a culture through specific, tangible, and sustainable behaviors. This is ethics with a small "e" and the decencies that this book suggests will ready an organization to adhere to the regulatory requirements in a hopeful, not cynical, context. Joseph L. Badaracco, Jr., the author of *Leading Quietly*, suggests that, "Sometimes it's the smallest acts that influence other people months or even years later. These are the behaviors that in a postcompliance world will lead to good citizenship, stewardship, profit, and success, no matter where in the world an organization operates."

THE BUSINESS WORLD AND ITS STRESSES

Heavy-handed regulation isn't the only challenge businesses face. The good times of the late twentieth century are over. The advantages enjoyed by the United States are no longer unchallenged. Much of the world is able to produce our products—either as competitors or as our outsourced partners. Workers in Japan, India, and other places are more educated than ever before, and often better educated than the average American. If we are going to compete, it will have to be done on the basis of innovation and teamwork.

The technology we thought would save us didn't. There are real benefits to technology, yet it is technology that makes the world the global marketplace that puts our jobs at risk. We no longer just ship our low-end jobs overseas. Doctors in India and Malaysia read our X-rays. Experts in developing countries process insurance claims and do our tax work. We buy our cars, medical equipment, and microchips from the worldwide marketplace.

To this brew add the following:

- Short-term glaring, constant inspection by the analysts on Wall Street, meaning pressure on profits on a quarterly basis
- A growing spirit of activism among shareholders
- The incredibly fast pace of change some call "aerobic innovation," and that's just to survive!
- Delayered, reengineered organizations where managing is important but leadership is critical

This is the new workplace context. The quiet office with an in-box and an out-box are gone forever; the nine-to-five job is hard to find; the "gold watch" retirement party is a relic of a different time. The traditional organization chart has been replaced by a boundaryless network that is more about the white spaces than the lines connecting the boxes.

All these dynamics contribute to a business environment in which lifetime employment is a thing of the past. But is loyalty between employers and employees obsolete as well? Not quite, says David Noer, consultant and author of *Healing the Wounds*, but it's not the same loyalty that typified much of corporate America in the 1950s.

Today, the average worker can expect to have 11 job changes and multiple careers, according to the U.S. Department of Labor. Both employers and employees understand that business is too dynamic to make long-term promises. That understanding works both ways. Mostly gone is the stigma that was once associated with employees losing or changing jobs. Loyalty in this environment is about a mutual commitment to a team, a project, or a learning opportunity. What, then, is the unwritten but understood covenant between employers and employees? In

"Creating a New Employment Contract," Noer neatly codifies many of these changes in his hypothetical "contract," and I am grateful that he has given me permission to reprint it here.

Creating a New Employment Contract

This firm exists in a rapidly changing world and a new employment contract has emerged between us as an organization and you as an employee. Listed below are some of the more important elements of that implicit contract:

1. Your hard work and contributions to this organization are treasured and appreciated, but we offer no guarantee of lifetime employment. Indeed, from time to time your role may be made tenuous when our firm is buffeted by national and global competition, and by the constant changes that characterize the marketplace at large.

2. While we cannot assure you of a job for life, you are in a rather good position to the extent that you possess (and continue to cultivate) key skills and experiences that are useful in our core businesses. In that case, we will view you as a "keeper" and will make special efforts to hang onto you.

3. The key skills [we require of you] will evolve and change over time as we respond to the turbulence of our contemporary world and as you grow in your career. Neither you nor we will always know in advance what those winning skills are, or are likely to be.

4. An important element of success in this new environment lies in a shared commitment to your continued

growth and development. In that regard, it is important to state up front that we consider your growth and your career to be your responsibility. You are in charge of making certain that you obtain the learning and experience needed to be successful.

For our part, as long as you are with us and adding value, we pledge to invest significantly in your continued development, to provide opportunities for you to move frequently into versatile assignments that will foster learning and enhance your personal value as well as your ability to contribute to the success of the enterprise. We will strive to provide relative freedom of choice, exposure to experience requiring a broad base of transferable skills, and a significant amount of mentoring and coaching.

5. Upwardly-mobile promotions will, quite frankly, be more infrequent and spaced further apart than in the past; but we will offer lateral movement into challenging positions that will stimulate learning and keep you from becoming bored.

6. Our relationship exists in a free-market, laissez-faire employment economy where change is the name of the game. Lifetime careers are still possible here but they are no longer the norm, and in most cases are not mutually desired. We should both acknowledge this reality up front.

    a. Therefore: If the time comes that you identify a better employment opportunity elsewhere, we would see it in your educated and enlightened self-interest to pursue it.

    b. Similarly, should the situation arise where your skills, abilities, and/or services are no longer seen as contributory or adding value to the organization, we will release you. When such moves occur at our initiative, we will make every effort to help you bridge the transition with severance pay, outplacement counseling, and other services designed to minimize the disruption of your life by enhancing your ability to land on your feet in a new setting. Here again, however, there are no guarantees.

7. If and when you move on to a new venture, it is our fervent desire that we go our separate ways with feelings of mutual respect and goodwill. Further, we hope to part knowing that at some point in our futures there might again come a time when there is a productive match between your skills and our organizational needs, and that both you and we might welcome the opportunity to reconnect around meaningful work.

8. Your career future may include a transition to a comparable organization or to one that differs greatly in size and/or context. Perhaps you will leave to create a business of your own. In any case, it is our sincere desire that your experience and learning with us will contribute significantly to continued success in whatever endeavors the future might hold for you.

9. As long as you are with us, we will work diligently to inspire you with a meaningful corporate vision and challenging tasks. We will strive to engage you with participative involvement and a genuine commitment

to quality in our products and services. In return, we expect your enthusiastic and committed best effort toward our shared values and work objectives.

10. You can expect that we will work you hard, pay you well, and energize your development through meaningful work and stimulating assignments. We commit to the difficult task of effective performance management, not the least part of which is a periodic, honest, and relevant performance review. Our aim is to scrupulously match performance with both pay and developmental opportunity.

11. We are aware that this is not the employment contract that either you or we were raised to expect. On the other hand, we think it represents an accurate and fair reflection of the realities of today's circumstances. We commit ourselves to making the elements of this contract work, and look for a similar commitment from you.

Within this context, work-life balance has become an oxymoron. Former Secretary of Labor Robert Reich wrote, "There's no relaxing, no cruise control, no resting on your laurels or seniority . . . You're either on the fast track or you're not . . . Sure, it's easier than ever to work part-time, go on a long vacation, or take a year or several to be at home with a new child. But beware. If you do any of these things, you'll pay a big price. Don't expect to get back on the fast track easily, because while you were gone too much will have happened, and other people will have moved in to take over."

We strive for balance in our workplaces, but too often we settle for less stress. In the face of these realities, I believe, and others believe as well, that commitment to cultural decency won't change the reality of work-life stress and imbalance, but it can be a tonic that can relieve the counterproductive effects of our commercial dynamism.

THE CEO'S DILEMMA

The CEO's dilemma is how to lead ethically in the face of all of these trends while also meeting the timeless requirements to perform, to win.

This dilemma is most eloquently posed by Harold Kushner in *Living a Life That Matters*: "Where will I find the inner strength to do what I know is right in the face of financial pressures to do otherwise?" The disarming reality is that the widely publicized, even melodramatized megacorporate scandals and the heavy-handed recent compliance laws have not necessarily made public companies behave more ethically.

Does the answer to avoiding ethical transgressions lie in even tougher laws? More draconian punishment? More specific ethics statements? Comprehensive compliance training? Those of us interested in living in a world with well-behaved organizations are selling ourselves short when we focus just on compliance. If we think those rules will make us behave more ethically, we are wrong. A heavy hand alone will just produce heavy-handedness.

The recipe for well-behaved organizations starts with institutionalized small gestures and decencies that, when *combined with* structural changes—laws, regulations, and governance—result in organizations we can be proud of.

The reality is that as long as businesses have to recruit from the human race, a certain percentage of people will abuse their freedom, take advantage of their peers, and be destructive of the shared resources. Accountability suggests that if you fail to use your responsibility in the service of the organization, then we will take the responsibility away from you. It becomes a question of membership in the organization. Governance lets the members of the organization know that the values of the organization demand accountability and how individuals who abuse their freedom will be confronted.

This short book is neither an ethics sermon nor a learned treatise on organizational life. It provides examples from people-oriented business leaders who were and are participants in the post-SOX world and a summary of the lessons learned. It is a reminder that the solutions to complex problems don't have to be complex.

3

Leadership, Culture, and Decencies

You control the thermostat for the climate in which we work. And, today's most sought-after benefit is integrity. Without integrity, you can never develop trust. Without trust, you will never develop people. Without people, you will never maintain a following. And without followers, you have no one to lead.

ANONYMOUS, AS QUOTED IN *LISTEN-UP LEADER*

I confess that until 10 years ago, the subject of leadership theory was barely on my radar screen.

The outplacement company whose name included my own had grown to a respectable size. But, as so often happens with prosperous companies, it had grown to a point where its needs placed new demands on the capacities of its leaders. For my company to reach the next level, I would have to go through a personal transformation. I had given Lee Hecht Harrison (LHH) the best I was capable of, but in retrospect, I realized that while I *managed* the firm's growth competently, I understood too little about *leadership*.

The firm's growth required me to provide a new level of leadership. It was a stretch goal for me. I set about learning all I could about leadership. I read and listened and watched with fascination. I met with leaders I admired and authors who are students of leadership. I asked myself, "Am I one of those?" "Am I enough of a leader?" "Do I have what it takes?"

Eventually I realized what every leader must come to accept. The quality of leadership is in the eye of the beholder. Leaders have followers. Managers have subordinates. I wanted followers. Subordinates can be enlisted; followers have to be earned. Following, after all, is a voluntary activity. I wanted to be the type of leader who inspired followers to live up to their highest standards and work together in the service of the organization.

I realize that my wish list sounds idealistic and rather emotional. But my decision to be more a leader than a manager was pragmatic. Managers have to direct and be accountable for specific outcomes. Leaders inspire people to find ways to fulfill not only their job descriptions, but also a greater role within the company. I learned that one reason the study of leadership—as opposed to management—emerged in the early 1990s was that many corporations had downsized their management ranks. Without the traditional layers of middle management, top executives simply had less time to manage the number of people under them.

But how would I know if my subordinates and peers had morphed into followers? It's not like people pass me in the hallway and say, "Good morning, Steve, and by the way, you really *are* a leader!" I wondered what is it that people associate with leadership. The term "charisma" often came up.

So I asked myself, "Do I have *charisma*? If I wasn't born with a sufficient quantity, how do I get more? Are there charisma-development programs anywhere?" I'd always believed that leaders were born that way. It was a DNA thing. Not so in the judgment of Warren Bennis, who argues that leadership derives from experiences, learning, and awareness—not biology. I heard from those who argued that charisma is indispensable and others who insisted that charisma can be counterproductive because it can obscure other more valuable leadership attributes. I listened to tapes from those who argued that leadership is especially challenging in a more virtual and team-oriented corporate world. And I listened to leaders who said they succeeded despite themselves.

I am therefore comfortable that even though I don't know for sure whether I am enough of a *leader*, I do know that I am a *learner* who can strive to be a leader. If I continue to listen and learn from people who teach leadership and from those who exhibit leadership, I'll grow *with* and *for* my company. My view of leadership will inevitably change over time, but for now I believe that leadership is associated with several characteristics, some of which I describe below.

A leader must be *credible*. Credibility derives from *competency*. A leader without the skills required to achieve the organization's mission simply can't get the job done. Some leaders are regarded so by virtue of their technical skills. In that case, they must be willing to transfer those skills. But all leaders need to be seen as competent.

Followers are inspired by leaders who display *energy*, *optimism*, and the ability to *galvanize* diverse talent. The knack of helping people win and then acknowledging them when they do succeed is important. At the same time, leaders must be *constructive*, *protective*, and *willing* to hold themselves and others accountable, even in the most nonhierarchical structures.

I have observed that many of the best leaders display *humility* rather than arrogance. Humility is not thinking less of yourself. It's thinking of yourself less often. A leader with humility understands that no single individual, not even the individual currently occupying the position of chief executive, can single-handedly create a great organization. Jim Collins, the author of *Good to Great,* proposes the following test of humility: "Do [potential leaders] have the proper relationship to the window and the mirror so that when talking about results, they point out the window, but when asked about screwups and things that went bad, they point to the mirror?"

Related to humility is the *desire to help people win.* That does not only mean sharing the credit. It also means setting achievable goals and giving people the resources and training they need to reach those goals. It means looking for what they do right; looking, as Boston Philharmonic conductor Benjamin Zander suggests, for the "A" in everyone. And sometimes it means *tough love*—a concept well understood by effective parents. Helping people win involves transferring your strength to them so that they can grow and succeed.

Courage is a virtue frequently associated with leadership. History books are filled with grand heroic acts of courage, so it is understandable if we think of courage in those terms. It's common to speak of courage as something that a leader *has.* I prefer to speak of courage as something that a leader *does.* That's why I prefer to contextualize the subject in terms of "acts of courage" or "moments of courage." Stated like this—we all have moments, we are all confronted by the need to act—people have countless opportunities to choose how and when they will display this attribute called *courage.*

In the spirit of small decencies, the acts of courage that impress me most are the ones that concern everyday encounters with colleagues, customers, and supervisors. Rarely are they of monumental consequence. But as surely as character is defined by choices, every such choice takes us beyond our previous experience and makes us trespass into dangerous neighborhoods beyond our comfort zone. "Courage is about making tough choices, but those choices more often than not involve the little things we do," say Jim Kouzes and Barry Posner in *A Leader's Legacy*.

Leadership also requires *energy, optimism,* and the gift of *creating an enabling* environment where innovators can succeed and failure is tolerated. No single leader will have all the attributes I've discussed all of the time; leadership is not about personal perfection. Instead, good leaders surround themselves with others who have the skills they lack. But there are two absolutely critical aspects of leadership that you can't leave to someone else. Those critical attributes are *purpose* and *integrity*.

Many leaders are blessed with a *vision* for their organization. At the minimum, as Colin Powell puts it, leaders have the ability to "see around corners." They advance a vision statement as a guide to the future direction of the organization. Everyone needs hope for the future. Visionary leaders provide this hope. Tom Peters believes that leaders "must create new worlds. And then destroy them; and then create anew." But visions need moral grounding, as well. "Visions that are merely proclaimed, but not lived convincingly are nothing more than mockeries of the process," he says. In their book *Leaders*, Warren Bennis and Burt Nanus describe visionary leaders as "creating dangerously. They change the basic metabolism of the organization. Leaders articulate and define what has previously remained implicit or unsaid; then they invent images, metaphors, and models that provide a focus for new attention. An essential factor in leadership is the capacity to influence and organize meaning for the members of the organization." By so doing, leaders consolidate or challenge prevailing wisdom.

Ironically, while being forward-looking is a highly valued leadership competence, it is often the one leaders are least capable of demonstrating. They are too often hostage to the present. "Today's leaders have to be concerned about tomorrow's world and those who will inherit it," write Kouzes and Posner in *A Leader's Legacy*. "Leaders must have the capacity to envision an uplifting and ennobling image of the future and to enlist others in a common purpose. That's the good news. The bad news is that today's leaders stink at it."

Here's a sampling of some of the ways leaders have expressed their visions.

- "When I'm through . . . everyone will have one."—Henry Ford on democratizing the automobile
- "I believe that this nation should commit itself to achieving the goal, before this decade is out, of landing a man on the moon and returning him safely to the Earth."—President John F. Kennedy, May 25, 1961
- "There's something going on here . . . something that is changing the world . . . and this is the epicenter." Steve Jobs of Apple Computers during its initial start-up
- "Quality, hard work, and commitment—the stuff America is made of. Our goal is to be the best. What else is there? If you can find a better car, buy it."—Lee Iacocca when he was chairman of Chrysler Corporation
- "2000 stores by the year 2000."—Howard Schultz of Starbucks Coffee Company

- "I have a dream that my four little children will one day live in a nation where they will not be judged by the color of their skin but by the content of their character."—Dr. Martin Luther King, Jr.

Purpose is sometimes expressed in a mission, sometimes in a values statement. If vision is conceptualizing what the future of the organization might be, *purpose* articulates the higher reason for being in the business in the first place. The most effective leaders are able to communicate how vision and purpose connect in a way that resonates with employees' need for meaning. Bennis and Nanus finish their discussion of vision by saying, "In short, an essential factor in leadership is the capacity to influence and organize meaning for the members of the organization." Chuck Schwab, the CEO of discount broker Charles Schwab & Co., defined the business: "Our employees see themselves as custodians of their customers' financial dreams." In this way, Chuck Schwab neatly links vision and purpose. There's nothing transactional about the definition of what is, after all, a transactional business. Leaders reach for the transformational whenever possible.

Lack of purpose is probably one of the principal challenges we face today. "Why does one inner city kid overcome circumstances and create a productive, fulfilling life, while others get caught up in a life of drugs and crime?" asks Kevin Cashman in *Leadership from the Inside Out*. In the outplacement world where I spend much of my time, why does one unemployed person view this situation as a hopeless disaster, while others see job loss as an opportunity to connect with something they've always wanted to do? "Why does a true leader see possibilities, while another sees only problems?" Cashman asks. My answer: Some people can find their purpose in even the most trying circumstances. To do so requires incredible strength of character. "Leadership is a potent combination of strategy and character," says General H. Norman Schwarzkopf. "But if you must be without one, be without the strategy."

And that leads us to the most indispensable leadership attribute: *integrity*. Integrity is based on honesty, openness, trustworthiness, and value-consciousness. Leaders who have integrity consistently model the behavior they advocate. They make sure that the words match the music. They operate on the DWYSYWD basis: Do What You Said You Would Do. Above all, they have a sense of ethics that trickles down through the organization.

Integrity is closely related to authenticity. Nothing can dismantle a leader's effectiveness as well as a whiff of hypocrisy can, and followers can smell it a mile away. Leaders have integrity when they align their actions with their statements and values. That's the first test of integrity, and in some ways it's the easiest. There are two other parts of the test, though. The second test of integrity is a willingness to articulate the standards and assumptions that drive the vision of integrity. The third test is a willingness to engage with those who might challenge some of those standards and assumptions, regardless of their power and status. With integrity comes trust and the confidence that leaders will do as they have promised.

TRUST: LEADERSHIP IN ACTION, NOT JUST ON PAPER

Trust is a fragile commodity in the world of business. It's hard to earn and easy to lose. Business has always had an uneasy relationship with trust. We say we want to trust each other, but if we look at what businesses actually do, we wouldn't believe it. What have organizations traditionally invested in? Locks, audits, guards, rules, regulations, permissions, and sign-offs. Command and control are difficult habits to break.

Nevertheless, if organizations are to prosper, a high level of trust is necessary. The costs of mistrust are simply too high, burdening every business process with friction and time. Trust is the glue for many essential business activities. At the heart of collaboration is trust. It is the baseline for employee empowerment, allowing every member of the team to participate fully.

Trust begins with the leader. Individuals who are unable to trust fail to become leaders because, unwilling to be dependent on others, others refuse to depend on them. Trust is not a passive attribute. The decision to trust often requires making wrenching choices.

Patrick Charmel, the president of Griffin Hospital in Derby, Connecticut, was faced with such a choice. In the dark days following the events of September 11, 2001, a bioterrorist still unknown released infectious anthrax into the postal system, killing five people. Ottilie Lundgren, age 94, became the fifth—and last—person to die of the deadly disease during a short-lived reign of terror. She apparently contracted anthrax through cross-contaminated mail. She was admitted to Griffin Hospital. Charmel came under significant pressure from the Federal Bureau of Investigation (FBI) to withhold information from employees (and the public) about the patient and her subsequent death. Yet he decided to inform 200 day-shift employees about the case, fully recognizing that it might make the issue public.

"Charmel knew the trust relationship that he'd been so instrumental in building depended on his credibility with employees," said Amy Lyman, cofounder of the Great Place to Work Institute. "The credibility had been built in his commitment to share information with employees about important issues affecting the organization, to be available to give answers to their questions, and to deliver on his promise to look out for their best interests," she says.

Trust often requires leaders to choose between two honorable paths. "My decision to tell employees was never in doubt even though it was personally difficult because it was in conflict with high-ranking FBI officials," Charmel said. "I could not violate or put in jeopardy the trust relationship Griffin and I have with our employees and the community." He understood that if he could trust his staff to make decisions that had life or death consequences for thousands of patients every year, he could trust them to act properly in this matter. A high level of trust makes such confidence possible. It's no accident that Griffin Hospital is one of the top 10 best places to work, according to the Great Place to Work Institute.

We know trust when we see it, but what exactly is trust? One of my Adecco colleagues, Reinhard K. Sprenger, is also one of Europe's most eminent management experts and the author of *Trust: The Best Way to Manage.* After describing how trust operates in commerce and organizations, Sprenger suggests that trust is a highly personal process experienced one person and one transaction at a time. Trust, according to Sprenger, exists when a person would say:

I am prepared to relinquish control of another person because I expect them to be competent, and to act with integrity and goodwill.

In terms of traditional management command and control theory, this definition of trust is liberating because it makes explicit the quality of being vulnerable. Trust is about sharing power. If you want to be trusted as a leader, you have to give some of your power away. The paradox is that by relinquishing some power, a leader gains even more. If you want something from someone, sometimes you first have to give it to them before they can give it back to you.

Although many leaders find it difficult to trust others, there's really no substitute for trust. The best way to have others trust you is for you to trust them first. Yes, that opens you up to betrayal. Yes, trust is the willingness to risk real harm. Yes, you may end up looking less like the invincible and indomitable leader you want everyone to see. But what's the alternative? Command and control simply don't work in flattened networked organizations filled with knowledge workers.

"If you don't trust, then what?" Kouzes and Posner ask in *A Leader's Legacy*. "Many things just won't get done. You're left with doing more and more work yourself. You're left with constantly checking up on other people's work, spending time micromanaging. You're left with getting less than the best from your team."

Nothing corrodes a corporate culture more than high-minded ideals published in statements being routinely, if inadvertently, violated by its leaders. It may actually be better if the organization did away with the pretense of publishing values. The organization may be corrupt, but at least it wouldn't be hypocritical.

When there is a disconnect between professed values and actual conduct, mission and values statements only breed cynicism and erode trust. As Tom Peters explains, if the ideas "are merely proclaimed, but not lived convincingly they are nothing more than mockeries of the process."

Under such conditions, the corporate culture starts to allow all types of self-destructive behaviors. Soon the sense of shared values deteriorates to such an extent that there are no checks on corporate conduct. Let me be clear. The problem is not in having ethical principles. The issue is leaders who suspend ethical norms when there appear to be costs to conforming to the ethical principles. We have all been tested by the pull of opportunism that is on a collision course with core values.

Values statements, ethics manuals, and codes of conduct do not inoculate organizations against bad behavior. Alas, while such documents are useful as reminders of values that have already been internalized, they are imperfect predictors of future behavior. Enron, the poster company for bad behavior, for example, actually had an ethics and compliance manual that it distributed with great pride to every employee. And it was a pretty good ethics manual, a model in some ways of what a comprehensive corporate ethics manual should be. You can still find these manuals for sale on eBay, symbols of how utterly irrelevant such manuals can be in the face of determined wrongdoing.

Unless the values statements are grounded by something other than fancy words and empty intentions, they have little or no power. One organization that has turned its values statement into an enduring standard that actually shapes individual and institutional behavior for the better is Johnson & Johnson. The Credo, as it is called at J&J, is the first thing visitors and employees see as they enter the marble lobby of the company's New Brunswick, New Jersey, headquarters. Literally carved in stone on a lobby wall, the Credo is a simple, one-page statement that for 70 years has guided the company's actions in fulfilling its responsibilities to customers, employees, the community, and stockholders.

But the Credo is not just reserved for visitors. If you visit offices throughout the company, and not just at headquarters, you will find that employees display the Credo on every available surface, from wall posters to desk calendars to coffee mugs.

The Credo speaks both loudly and quietly at every level of Johnson & Johnson. The company has systematically embedded the Credo into the company's DNA to such an extent that it is sometimes difficult to determine if the company drives the Credo or the Credo drives the company. In the beginning Robert Wood Johnson wisely annunciated the Credo as a set of values. Not as goals, because goals don't have a moral dimension. Moreover, goals can be attained, and then what? Johnson understood that people need not goals, but standards. Standards help managers lead companies to greatness day by day. They stand up and proclaim: Here's what we stand for; here's how we stand apart; and this is where we stand together. As the syndicated business columnist Dale Dauten observes in *The Gifted Boss*, "One standard is worth a thousand committee meetings."

Johnson & Johnson has taken two specific actions to make the Credo a living force. The first action is the company's willingness to reconstruct the Credo to meet contemporary needs. By doing this, the company sends an unmistakable signal that the Credo is not just the property of the executives but that it belongs to everyone. The company has also used a process called the Credo Challenge, wherein senior management is encouraged to grapple with the meaning of the Credo. This process has been highly effective in getting managers around the world to take ownership of its values and wrestle with inconsistencies between company actions or policies and the Credo.

Many other businesses actually undermine the trust they want to build by instituting ill-conceived policies. Here's an example of what I mean. Scott Cawood, who served as vice president for global talent at Revlon, tells this story. "I was visiting a retail company that had placed several colorful posters on the wall by the front desk. The posters highlighted the five core principles of the entire organization—with the word 'trust' at the top of the list. Yet, whenever people entered and exited the building, guards in blue uniforms inspected their bags and briefcases. The most important principle of the organization was being broken each time an employee entered or left the building. These types of inconsistent messages—saying one thing but doing another—erode trust and trigger an instant disconnect."

This retail company with the security guards can take a lesson from Wal-Mart. Later in this chapter, I discuss the Wal-Mart greeter gesture as a small decency that morphed into a company policy: having an employee at the door greeting customers. While this program's main goal is to distinguish Wal-Mart from other retailers by making shoppers feel welcome, Sam Walton also understood that it discouraged shoplifters. Of course, a security guard at the front of each store would have performed the same function, but he didn't want to intimidate the majority of honest customers just to send a signal to the small number of crooks.

Have you ever been a guest at a hotel where everything was secured to a wall and even the hangers had that funny hardware that made them useless if taken home? I don't know about you, but I don't think you should treat guests like that. In fact, most hotel surveys indicate that customers resent being treated as if they were thieves. Ritz-Carlton has the right idea: it treats its customers as trusted guests from the time they check in, including furnishing room closets with high-quality wooden and silk clothes hangers. This is a decency that pays off with customer loyalty. And, by the way, the hotel is not naive.

It knows that some hangers will be removed. But when a guest removes a hanger, the hotel treats the incident as a purchase rather than a theft. Discrete signs at the Ritz and other hotels invite guests who enjoy an amenity, whether it be a clothes hanger, towel, or bathrobe, to take them. A charge will appear on their bill at checkout. Instead of paying lip service to one set of values and operating by another, Ritz-Carlton molds its policies precisely around its values. Actions such as these reinforce the values and build, not diminish, trust at every level of the enterprise.

CORPORATE CULTURES

Corporate culture is a set of messages concerning how people operate in an organization. It provides the answer to the question, "How do we do things around here?" While it may be hard to define or measure an organization's culture, it is somewhat easier to grasp the "climate" or attitudinal feel of the place. This is what we sense in a restaurant or retail store or doctor's office; it is what we experience within the first few minutes after entering a new business, or even a particular department. Sometimes we can't put our finger on what we're experiencing, but we all know the feeling of walking into a new space and immediately feeling welcomed or alienated. It is our overall sense of the place, and it shapes our expectations of what's to come from our interactions with the people there. Culture is a feeling so strong that it is even measurable with surveys. Leadership expert Ed Lawler, puts it bluntly: "How people are treated increasingly determines whether a company will prosper and even survive."

The term *corporate culture* was coined by Terrence E. Deal and Allan A. Kennedy in their book *Corporate Culture*. Their work demonstrates the inevitable link between effective leadership and building a cohesive culture. They say in their follow-up book, *The New Corporate Cultures*, that this is leadership that not only allows the company to fulfill its economic mission but also, "It is leadership that seeks to shape a working environment that people at all levels can identify with. It is leadership that encourages leadership from everyone. It is leadership that is not afraid to stand for something. It is leadership that cares about a myriad of details that make a company work."

Decencies serve the culture by adding "stickiness" to ethical behaviors. The resulting culture promotes and rewards certain behaviors, while underscoring transgressions, boundaries, and taboos to be avoided. Culture in an organization is constructed by its membership, one gesture at a time. It is built incrementally and changes slowly and methodically. Leaders have an amplified role in this process because their actions are more visible than those of others.

Many describe corporate culture as the "glue" that holds a company made of diverse people together. The Johnson & Johnson Credo, for example, is often referred to as the glue that binds together the corporation's 200 operating companies around the world. David Noer, author of *Healing the Wounds: Overcoming the Trauma of Layoffs and Revitalizing Downsized Organizations*, knows what it takes to cultivate highly motivated workplace cultures. In "A Recipe for Glue," he lists the ingredients and attitudes required to cultivate productive teamwork in an environment of decency and respect that is truly focused on the needs of the customers.

A Recipe for Glue

Fill glue pot with the fresh, pure, clear water of undiluted human spirit.

Take special care not to contaminate with preconceived ideas or to pollute with excess control.

Fill slowly; notice that the pot only fills from the bottom up. It's impossible to fill it from the top down.

Stir in equal parts of customer focus and pride in good work.

Bring to boil and blend in a liberal portion of diversity; one part self-esteem; and one part tolerance.

Fold in accountability.

Simmer until smooth and thick, stirring with shared leadership and clear goals.

Season with a dash of humor and a pinch of adventure.

Let cool, then garnish with a topping of core values.

Serve by coating all boxes in the organization chart, with particular attention to the white spaces. With proper application, the boxes disappear and all that can be seen is productivity, creativity, and customer service.

THE GRIP OF CHANGE

Organizations everywhere are in the grip of change. Time compression is affecting every dimension of business: speed of change, speed of new product development, speed of obsolescence, and speed of structural transformation. Although the evolution of corporate culture may be the most critical predictor of corporate success, it sometimes seems that we accept culture as an exception to the speed with which everything else in business changes. Culture is not an exception. We should think of it in step with the other forces that shape our organizations.

We have learned to accept the traditional view that cultures do indeed develop incrementally over time as traditions are born and stories are told. Today's leaders simply can't afford that slow pace. Conscious, proactive, intentional culture shaping is the new order of the day. Everything else—innovation, globalization, technology, regulation—is moving too fast. Corporate culture, which is a critical enabler of all other business activities, simply can't lag behind. I believe that leaders can and should accelerate cultural development through decencies.

I'm not saying that it's easy to "fix" a problematic culture and create a supportive, productive, ethical or compliant climate. It's really hard work—maybe the hardest part of a leader's job. I am saying that you don't have to sit back and wait for culture change. You can start by making little things happen in your immediate surroundings. If the "little things" (small but meaningful gestures) take hold and become pervasive, they create stories and patterns and texture that can enrich a culture. These little things have power because they can be felt every day by everyone. They become a unifying experience that becomes sustainable by the force of everyone repeating them. You've sped up the cultural evolutionary process.

Organizations need to have cultures in which people feel included, safe, respected, trusted, connected, recognized, and acknowledged as valued. In a way, this isn't really asking much from the place where we invest the most productive years of our lives. Creating and proactively influencing culture is a leadership imperative.

THE STEWARDSHIP OF ETHICAL CULTURE

Two of the discussions taking place in the professional literature about leadership and its relationship to culture are worth mentioning. One has to do with the kinds of leadership that various cultures support—what kind of leadership is good when you're working in France or Japan, for example, or on Wall Street or at a Silicon Valley start-up. For our purposes, this is not critical because most cultures support and respond to leadership behaviors that are high on integrity, encouragement, and fairness. So, in this sense, what we're talking about here is quite universal.

The other line of thinking has to do with stewardship, and this is critical for leaders who want a culture of decencies to flourish. *Stewardship* is the willingness of leaders to be accountable for the well-being of the larger institution by operating in service of rather than in control of workers. It begins with the willingness to be accountable for some larger purpose than ourselves. It requires the eagerness to treat workers as colleagues and partners. Stewardship bets on local solution and control. It assumes that the worker closest to the customer is in the best position to be accountable and is central to making meaningful change possible. It rejects the concept of caretaking and insists that accountability be chosen.

This is a radical thought. A whole industry has grown up around Sarbanes-Oxley and related regulatory mandates focused exclusively on one thing: intensifying an organization's ability to guarantee compliance. But as we saw in Chapter 2, even the regulators found that regulations do not guarantee compliance.

When the regulators came to the conclusion that what was also needed was a focus on ethical culture, I think they approached this idea of accountability, of stewardship. I'm not sure they know the full power of the discussion they started. When regulators are asked about what they mean by an "ethical culture," it's obvious that their imaginations are limited. It's almost like the censor's self-serving definition of pornography: "We know it when we see it." When regulators are pushed to describe what they mean by "ethical culture," they refer to rules, codes, regulations, HR policies, and compensation practices. This is simply not helpful enough.

I believe it's more telling to define *ethical culture* as the sum of the tangible, homegrown, specific behaviors, norms of reciprocity, and time-honored traditions that form the fabric of an organization, help ensure its sustainability, and help reduce its vulnerability. These are the behaviors and attitudes that, together, help members of the organization construct and enforce standards of how people will act. They allow people within the organization to say to themselves, "This is how we do things here," or, as the case may be, "That's *not* how we do things around here." Another term for these behaviors is "small decencies."

Herb Kelleher used much more than a book of corporate policies and procedures to create Southwest Airlines, "the airline that love built." The stories are endless of the Kelleher-led behaviors that form the unique—and highly effective—Southwest culture. The late Ken Iverson, chairman and CEO of Nucor, Inc., introduced behaviors that are credited with sustaining America's only consistently profitable steel company. These behaviors were all filtered through Iverson's commitment to an organizationally flat, nonhierarchical, and unpretentious atmosphere.

These examples and others like them serve as insight into the indispensable power of culture as potential preventive medicine against corporate misconduct. They demonstrate how small decencies are the building blocks that set the tone for an organization which provides connectivity to its people and a *raison d'etre*, why we come to the office in the morning. Most importantly, the examples show how decencies create an atmosphere where integrity and forthrightness can provide a protective shield from wrongdoing. These examples almost—but not quite—make compliance law more digestible.

The bridge between the codes of conduct, values statements, and performance reviews cited by regulators and a true ethical culture is effective leadership like that provided by Kelleher and Iverson. No one can legislate integrity. The best we can do is invest in leaders who set direction, create vision and strategy and goals, and perhaps even create a "learning organization." But even leaders capable of "walking the talk," who are inspirational to those immediately around them, are remote figures to the many more workers who do not encounter them on a day-to-day basis. Is a CEO's signature on a code of conduct or values statement enough to forge a culture of integrity, compliance, and respect? My experience, and the history of post-Sarbanes-Oxley corporate behavior, is that it is not.

A compliance-ready culture can't happen by itself. Yet it has to happen nonetheless because the stakes are so high. We simply must find a way to give organizations the best possible shot at succeeding.

TWO LEVERS: SMALL AND BIG DECENCIES

What each leader and manager can do is to initiate a kind of positive cycle with small gestures that help define the larger climate. The climate in turn stimulates more small gestures that make work life both better and more productive. To start this cycle, leaders model the gestures—ideally replicable and scalable—that can create a more ready foundation for a compliant culture.

Are small decencies sufficient by themselves to build ethical cultures? Maybe in some cases, or maybe over a long enough time frame. Fortunately, leaders have another lever to create culture change, and that's employing "big" decencies. Big decencies take two basic forms. First, there are the decencies that start small but then quickly take on a life of their own and morph into something more ambitious—more programmatic and standard.

The Wal-Mart greeter is a good example of this phenomenon. Can we leave aside for a moment all the criticisms of Wal-Mart and agree that there is something decent about the notion of a store representative who, with a smiling "Welcome" button, greets individual customers as they come in, assisting them with a shopping cart, and appreciating them for their business? The Wal-Mart greeter really signals something about trust, even as it serves a hardheaded business function.

The greeter program started out as a small decency. As Wal-Mart founder Sam Walton describes in his autobiography, *Sam Walton: Made in America,* the concept emerged from a visit he made to a store in Crowley, Louisiana. Walton noticed that the store manager stood in front of the building greeting customers. He was very impressed by this gesture, which he instinctively felt distinguished his store from others by making customers feel warm and welcome.

Walton took this small decency and made it into a big decency. The Wal-Mart greeter is now a mandated program. Every Wal-Mart store in the world has adopted the practice. I'm told that in Japan, the Wal-Mart greeter is somewhat of a celebrity, so powerful is its symbolic value to a culture that resonates with hospitality rituals. As a big decency, the greeter program has, no doubt, a program manager and a training budget. These days, it has become so institutionalized and expected that it is probably no more a decency than other store practices common to the franchise, such as having cashiers move from behind their point-of-sale terminals to stand in front of their aisles to welcome shoppers to the checkout.

Other decencies are big from conception. Any gesture that from the very beginning costs money, breaks existing rules, or requires specific participation of others within the organization is a big decency. Some big decencies are bigger than others. On a modest scale would be the decision by Ritz-Carlton to furnish its guests rooms with the coat hangers discussed earlier. The coat hangers had to be sourced, paid for, and inventoried. The chain had to implement a system for distributing the hangers and accounting for them. Signs had to be printed informing the guests that they were welcome to take the hangers for a fee. As far as programs go, this may not be very expensive, but it is nevertheless not a small decency.

At the other end of the scale are such decencies as Nucor's scholarship program, in which the company established a fund to help educate the children of employees. Other examples in this category include the creation of the Levi Strauss Foundation. (Of course, anything with the word "foundation" in it is, by definition, a big decency.) The Levi Strauss Foundation makes a donation of $500 to community groups in which an employee actively participates. For instance, if an employee serves on the board of a not-for-profit organization such as the American Heart Association, the company will give that organization a grant of $500 if its budget is up to $100,000, $1,000 for a budget between $100,000 and $1 million, and $1,500 for budgets of more than $1 million.

Another big decency that reinforces an individual employee's role as a volunteer is Salesforce.com's expectation that every employee donate 5 percent of his or her workday to community organizations. This San Francisco-based developer of customer relationship management software also supports a foundation with 1 percent of the firm's profits every year. These two gestures, one organized on an individual level and the other organized on a corporate scale, complement one another and demonstrate Salesforce.com's commitment. Some programs are grand decencies with substantial budgets behind them. Yet, like countless other corporate social responsibility programs, they help to create a corporate culture based on organizational values.

While leaders have at their disposal both small and big decencies, I believe it is impossible to effect culture change with big decencies alone. Big decencies without small decencies underpinning them lose much of their impact. Think about a carpet. It's a well-known fact that a key to making carpets desirable is the carpet pad. Although the pad is never seen, its presence is fundamental. Without a pad, even the most luxurious carpet feels flatter and, worse, actually suffers in terms of durability. Small decencies are to big decencies what a carpet pad is to carpet.

Part Two
Small Decencies in Action

Part Two describes small decencies that others have put to work successfully. Small decencies, as offered by working people every day, spring authentically from an individual's desire to treat others with humanity and respect. As you consider which decencies to try first, start with the ones that come naturally to you. If one feels too contrived, move on to another. Remember, not all decencies are appropriate for every practitioner or every work environment. Some will fit with your organization; others will not.

I have not personally tested all the decencies listed here. Some seem to me more compelling than others. But all have been tested at one organization or another, and the reports I received indicated that, in at least that one environment, they put the offering individual's—and, importantly, the organization's—values into action. It's on that basis that I describe the decencies.

I've grouped the decencies by interlocking themes: respect and consideration for others; recognition of employee efforts; humility in leadership; and listening. There's also a chapter about small decencies associated with the separation process, for it is at difficult times like these when people show their true colors and when decencies are most needed.

4

Consideration Decencies

The motto of successful CEOs: People first, strategy second.

RAM CHARAN, *BOARDS AT WORK*

When I started my professional career in 1964, my first office was next to the switchboard operator. Our spaces were separated by a glass window. In turn, the reception desk was separated from the waiting area by another glass window. From my office, I could see right past the receptionist into the waiting area.

I had recently been authorized to make purchases up to a modest sum. The manufacturing operation needed some office supplies, so the eager local area salespeople couldn't wait for an opportunity to be a supplier. The first one arrived on a Monday morning. He announced himself and sat down in the waiting area. He was right on time, and the receptionist dutifully announced that I had a visitor. By coincidence, Warren, the plant manager, arrived at the same time the office supply rep did. Meanwhile, I had been opening my mail when the announcement came, and I decided to finish that task. I figured 10 minutes wasn't too long for him to wait for my business.

The plant manager noticed the patiently waiting salesperson. He turned on his heel and came into my office.

"Steve, who is that guy in the reception area?"

"Oh, he's just a salesman," I said as I slit open an envelope.

The plant manager went into a rage. "Just a salesman? Have you ever been a salesman, Steve? Have you ever felt the rejection these guys have to go through every day? Do you know how excited he must be for this sales opportunity? Well, I was once a salesman, and I know how it feels to be insulted," he said.

"I don't mean to insult him," I said. I was young and defensive.

"But you did," he said. "Whether you realize it or not, by making him wait, you are telling him he is unimportant and is a low priority in your life. We do not insult people in this company, especially not our guests. Now, drop what you're doing, go out there, and invite him in to do your business."

Lesson learned. In the 42 subsequent years of my career, I have never consciously kept a visitor or guest, including salespeople, waiting. Whether or not you buy from a sales rep is not the issue. But receiving people promptly is a decency that counts because it is courteous and respectful of their time. The receptionist and your colleagues will notice this respect, and believe me, so will the salesperson. Salespeople talk, and they have large networks, including potential customers and employees. What do you want your organization's reputation to be?

RESPECT COMES FIRST

I define *respect* as consideration for self and of others. At a minimum, respect implies consideration for other people's privacy, their physical space and belongings, and, most of all, their time. It also calls for respect for different viewpoints, philosophies, physical ability, and beliefs. More importantly, respect means treating others as if you recognize their inherent worth and act on the assumption that they have something valuable to contribute.

The most basic decencies are those that demonstrate respect and consideration. A simple "hello" at the start of the day and "goodbye" at the end of the day are obvious but sometimes overlooked forms of respect. Failing to greet someone as you walk by is akin to not recognizing them as members of the community. Even when employees in organizations are called upon to do more with less, spending just a few minutes chatting can open lines of communication and set a positive tone for the day.

Remembering the names of the people you work with regularly is equally as important as saying hello. There is no sound sweeter to most people than their own names, and our ability to acknowledge those names is a supreme decency. Why do so many of us have trouble with it?

There is no environment more hierarchical, or more stressful, than medical residency programs. At the University of Washington, two third-year residents in surgery, perhaps the most hierarchical discipline in medicine, launched a friendly one-on-one competition to see which of them could learn the names of more nurse's aides, custodians, and transport and dietary staff and then use them authentically. Their goal was to break down the tradition of doctors acting with indifference to the other people who make hospitals function. Their unexpected reward was a support base that would do anything for them and for the patients they treat.

HALLWAY GREETINGS

When I'm asked to contrast work cultures in the United States and Europe, I often use this example: In the United States, if we meet people at work for the first time, we shake their hands and greet them as the newcomers they are. But then something changes. If we encounter the same people the next day, the emphasis shifts to making them feel less like newcomers than accepted members of the team. So we tend not to shake their hands again, because that's how newcomers are treated.

In Switzerland, at least, there is another convention. When I spend a week at Adecco's headquarters in Zurich, I often meet people at the beginning of my stay. The greeting is genuine, enthusiastic, and accompanied by a firm handshake. But if I encounter these same people in the next few days, I find it extraordinary that they usually approach me and shake my hand and inquire about my stay as if our relationship is starting over for the first time. I treasure these reassuring encounters. There's something powerful about regarding each meeting as an opportunity to start a relationship over again.

WORDS AT WORK

The decision as to what term we choose to apply to the community of people who work with us is itself a decency. Wal-Mart calls its employees "associates" as does W.L. Gore. Adecco, which calls people on staff "colleagues," avoids the term "temps" when speaking of the individuals it sends out on assignments. At Adecco, these people are associates, as well. Pfizer people from the chairman on down are all "colleagues." At Starbucks, everyone is referred to as "partners." At JetBlue, all employees from the president to flight attendants are "crew members." JetBlue takes the concept one step further. When you ask the top crew member how many passengers JetBlue carries, the answer is zero. People who fly JetBlue are customers. Customers are served; passengers are hauled. JetBlue is committed to acting as a customer service company that happens to fly airplanes.

THE COFFEE CONNECTION

John Sifonis, a former executive at Cisco Systems, had a practice of picking up a cup of coffee from Starbucks before going up to his Houston office. Every once in a while he picked up a cup for his administrative assistant, who was thrilled every time it happened. He didn't do it often enough for it to become routine or, worse, an entitlement. And Sifonis was careful not to deliver the cup of coffee only when he wanted to reward the administrative assistant for a particular job well done. There are, he knew, better ways to compensate employees for excellent performance. The practice of spontaneously delivering a cup of coffee was a decency meant only to convey how honored Sifonis was to have the colleague's assistance.

BIRTHDAY GREETINGS

Jim Donald, CEO and president of Starbucks, starts work at around 6 a.m. for one main reason. It's the time he reaches out to the people on the Starbucks team. He uses a variety of channels, including voice mail, e-mail, and handwritten thank you notes, to engage about 25 "partners" every day. But what got my attention is Donald's practice of, once a month, personally signing 500 birthday cards. Everyone at headquarters gets one from Donald every year. This year he will sign more than 3,500 birthday cards. One can argue this is a small decency verging on a big decency. After all, Donald relies on his assistant to keep track of the birthdays. But to me, his investment of large quantities of time to acknowledge birthdays signals a decency that few other CEOs of similar-sized organizations emulate.

REACHING OUT OF THE CORNER OFFICE

There are many occasions to demonstrate that you see coworkers as individuals. Some of these occasions are happy, such as a wedding, the birth of a child, or a child's graduation from high school or college. Gifts are not always necessary; a congratulatory phone call or quick note is a small decency that carries the same message of consideration.

Managers may also want to reach out to colleagues and subordinates when things aren't going so well. Tina Gordon, executive director of corporate communications at Johnson & Johnson, recalls that former CEO Jim Burke (on whose watch the Tylenol poisoning occurred) called her at home in the days after she broke her leg in a car accident. "Why didn't anyone tell me about this earlier?" Burke told her. "I'm concerned about you." More than a decade later, after surgery for cancer, Tina opened the very first get well card that arrived. It was from Ralph Larsen, who succeeded Burke as Johnson & Johnson's chief executive. Far from being anomalies, these examples are consistent with the way executives at Johnson & Johnson interact with people, and, importantly, with the way employees like Tina treat other people. Expressing concern for each other is simply part of the culture of this company that aims to be known as "the company that cares" by the customers it serves.

WELCOMING GUESTS

Few gestures make visitors to an organization feel more welcome than seeing their names displayed in the lobby. Whether the approach is low tech (a hand printed sign on an easel) or multimedia (an electronic monitor with moving text and graphics), seeing your name in the visitor's area makes you feel especially welcome.

If you're going to welcome guests in this fashion, just be thoughtful about two things. First, make sure you have the correct spelling of the names of the guests. Double-check to be sure you have them right.

Second, remember that some matters require discretion. A company wouldn't announce the visit of a competitor if merger talks were taking place. Here's another example of how a welcoming decency can go wrong and wind up on the evening news. The Transportation Security Authority often books hotel conference rooms for training federal air marshals, the people who go out of their way to be anonymous to make aviation safer. So imagine the agents' chagrin as they approached their hotel and saw printed in big block letters on the marquee in front of the hotel, "Welcome Federal Air Marshals." The moral of this story: any decency carried to a thoughtless extreme can become a liability.

Luckily, there's an easy way to avoid mistakes in this area. If you're not sure, ask. Ask even if you think you're sure. It's not about the surprise. It's about the effort you take to make others feel welcome.

DIRECTIONAL DECENCY

When a job applicant receives an invitation to interview at W.L. Gore & Associates, the information package includes a

Google map with the starting point of the applicant's home address and the Gore office as the destination. The map lays out the best route to the office and estimates the time required for the travel. It's just an additional gesture to reduce stress at a time when most applicants are nervous. Little gestures like this make a huge difference to the applicants. Ironically, W.L. Gore is helping the candidate offer his or her first decency to those in the company. By not getting lost and arriving on time, the candidate is respecting the time constraints of the interviewer. This is just one example of how one gesture of decency leads to others.

GLOBAL PERSPECTIVE

Here's another decency to do with a map, but this one is about demonstrating the value of people in other parts of the world. David Abney, president of UPS International, believes a global perspective is not only good business, but is also a decency when it reminds people that there's a big world out there that doesn't necessarily revolve around any particular country.

Abney is responsible for UPS's growing international delivery business. When you enter his office, you expect to find a big map of the world, and you won't be disappointed. But if you look closer, this map is different. The map has the hemispheres reversed. The Northern Hemisphere is at the bottom and the Southern Hemisphere is at the top. Moreover, in the center of the map, where one might expect to find the United States, sits the continent of Africa. The United States is represented, of course, but in the remote corner occupied in most maps by Australia and Micronesia. "The arrangement commands attention because it emphasizes how much of the world's land mass is concentrated in Africa, Europe, and Asia," Abney says.

"People often ask why I have a map configured in that way," Abney continues. "I tell them it's to remind me, and anyone who comes into my office, that although the U.S. is one of the world's largest economies and countries, there's a big world out there that doesn't revolve around the U.S."

The power of this approach is that by rearranging the artifacts in one's office, one challenges assumptions and stereotypes that narrow one's perspective and restrict innovation. As a decency, it sends a signal that there is fresh, welcoming thinking going on. Imagine how empowered such a map might make a visitor from another country feel. What can you do to arrange artifacts in your office to signal that you are open to new perspectives and fresh ways of relating to the world?

AVOID SLANG, IDIOMS, COLLOQUIALISMS

While we're on the topic of consideration for people from countries other than our own, I want to mention a decency related to language. When speaking to people whose first language is not your own, assume your audience will not understand slang, idioms, and colloquialisms. English is my first language. I frequently address audiences made up of people whose first language is French, German, Spanish, or another language. I am always grateful that they have made an effort to learn my language. I try to return that gratitude by being thoughtful about my phraseology. For example, instead of saying something is "old hat," I will say it is "familiar." I also try to avoid metaphors that require specific knowledge an audience may not have. For example, the phrase, "We're rounding third base and heading for home," is very evocative, but it requires an understanding of the game of baseball to be useful. Most Europeans and Africans, for example, would have no idea of what I was talking about.

WORK GROUP INTIMACY

Rita Bailey, the author of *Destination Profit*, tells of a manager of a rapidly growing department. When the department reached 150 people, the manager was concerned that growth threatened the close working relationships that had made the department so successful. His response was to place the photos of everyone in the department on a long bulletin board in the central hallway. As new employees came on board, their photos joined the faces already posted so that they could be easily recognized as part of the team.

OPEN UP DEPARTMENTAL MEETINGS

It's critical that departments run efficiently, but too often organizations shortchange themselves by forgetting that departments also need to work together for the sake of the customer. At Metso Minerals Industries, a York, Pennsylvania–based manufacturer of grinding products, departmental meetings are routinely opened up to representatives of other departments. Dawna Smeltzer, manager of aftermarket services at Metso Minerals Industries, makes it a point to invite other departments to her meetings. Sometimes she will invite representatives from such departments as engineering, purchasing, and finance to attend. The trick, she says, is to issue the invitations in person or by telephone. It takes longer, but it's much more effective than e-mail.

This kind of cross-departmental interaction breaks down the silo mentality that confounds so many organizations. The company has streamlined processes and avoided extra costs thanks to the cooperation. "Another benefit we have found is that it reduces gossip," Smeltzer says. "Gossip is almost always destructive," she says. "Anything that replaces unproductive conjecture with real facts is good for the company and the customer."

INTRODUCTIONS AT MEETINGS

Many meetings feel rushed because attendees often feel that they have more to do than they have time for. As a result, introductions are often given short shrift or dispensed with altogether in the service of getting to the action items. I think that's a mistake, not only because it may mean that a new person isn't recognized, but also because not knowing your coworkers inhibits efficient functioning. From time to time, teams, no less than any other corporate asset, need maintenance, and at such times introductions are no less an action item than anything else on the agenda.

Check out whether everyone in a meeting or group knows each other. Nothing distances a group from its purpose as much as some people operating without knowing each other's names. Even when participants have previously been introduced, another round of introductions is usually beneficial. Many people have difficulty remembering names, especially in a group setting (see below). For these people, a short round of introductions can be a real benefit.

Introductions can deliver more information than just names. Why not ask people to take turns saying what department they represent and one thing they are proud of having accomplished this week? This way individuals get a chance to be recognized, and the group gets some good information that might make the meeting go more smoothly.

You can be creative with introductions. Days later when the subject of the meeting is long forgotten, people will remember the introductions. Following are three ways to make introductions creative.

We've all been in large groups where people introduce themselves. It's frustrating because by the time the third person introduces himself or herself, the first name is forgotten. For meetings with up to 10 participants, here's a way to fix that problem. The first person says his or her name. "Peter Antonelli." Now, before the second person says his or her name, he or she repeats the name of the first person. "Peter Antonelli. And I'm Mary Raphael." The third person has to repeat the first two names before getting to his or her own. "Peter Antonelli. Mary Raphael. And I'm Joe Black." And so on. Believe me, by the end of the process, people will know each other's names.

For larger groups, here's another approach that I've found very effective. Instead of having participants introduce themselves, ask each to introduce the person to the right (or left). "This is Rachel James. Rachel has been with the company for 11 years, first as a quality assurance analyst, and now as team leader for the Qubic project." If necessary, take 60 seconds for people to introduce themselves to each other for this purpose.

At new employee orientation meetings at Lee Hecht Harrison, individuals rise to introduce themselves. But in addition to the standard introductory essentials (name, department, previous work, family, etc.), they are asked to tell the group one thing about themselves that few people are likely to know. This has resulted in people demonstrating just how interesting the human race is. I've had people volunteer that they are skydivers, bungee jumpers, and opera singers. The decency is that this detail allows people to think of each other in richer ways. It also creates better openings for conversations as people encounter each other after the orientation.

LIMIT ONE-HOUR MEETINGS TO 45 MINUTES

Like many executives, Jim Donald, CEO and president of Starbucks, resents the time consumed by endless meetings. His response? He insists that hour-long meetings be completed in 45 minutes. As a time management technique, this step saves eight hours a week. Saving time is great, but that's not what interests me. The decency is Donald's suggestion regarding what his team should do with the time savings. "I want you to take your extra 15 minutes to call someone you usually do not contact every day," he told *Fortune* magazine.

VOICE QUESTIONS, NOT OPINIONS

Sam Goldwyn, the movie mogul, once said: "I don't want any yes-men around me. I want them to tell me the truth, even if it costs them their jobs." The quote is humorous because we all know executives who have their minds made up and tolerate no dissent, despite their protestations to the contrary. Not being open to others' ideas shows a lack of respect; asking a question when you already have an answer is insincere and wastes the other person's time. Questions that are not questions are corrosive to a culture because smart people hesitate to offer an intellectual challenge. Here's the decency: if you really want to have the best decisions, start out with a question and state your opinion last. This way subordinates who have something to say will feel freer to offer their opinions.

I am not suggesting that leaders should not have opinions or, when it's appropriate, voice them. When there is a legal or safety issue at stake, for example, a leader's opinion must be stated forcefully. The decency is about being clear. Make a statement when you have made a decision. Ask a question only if you sincerely want to hear the opinions of others.

THE GOSSIP TRAP

Words matter. Your treatment of private information about others is basic consideration. Consideration also means no gossiping. There is a nineteenth-century Talmudic story about a man who spread gossip about the town's rabbi. Eventually, the man realized the error of his ways and went to the rabbi to ask for forgiveness. The rabbi told him that he would be forgiven if he performed one service. The man was to go home, take his favorite feather pillow from his bed, cut it up, and scatter the feathers to the wind. After he had done so, he should then return to the rabbi.

Though puzzled by this strange request, the man was happy to be let off with so easy a penance. He quickly cut up the pillow, scattered the feathers, and returned to the rabbi's house.

"Am I now forgiven?" he asked.

"Just one more thing," the rabbi said. "Go now and gather up all the feathers."

But the wind had scattered the feathers to the four corners of the earth. After searching for hours, the man returned with only three feathers in his hand.

"You see," said the rabbi, "once you spread gossip, you can never completely undo the wrong. And though you may truly wish to correct the evil you have done, it is as impossible to repair the damage done by your words as it is to recover the feathers. Your words are out there in the marketplace, spreading hate, even as we speak."

INVITE EMPLOYEES TO LUNCH

Invite each of your team members to lunch with you on a quarterly basis. The emphasis must be on the invitation. Employees must be free to decline. If an employee feels there may be repercussions at work for declining the invitation, then what you have is not a small decency but a meeting. The idea is to keep the invitation informal and unpredictable. If there's a list of employees and dates, you've already lost. Keep the lunch simple, preferably in the employee cafeteria or a brown bag sit-down in a public setting. A good question to ask is, "What do we need to do to keep you with us?"

5

Recognition Decencies

Don't worry when you are not recognized,
but strive to be worthy of recognition.

ABRAHAM LINCOLN

In *Destination Profit,* Scott Cawood tells of a vice president at a Manhattan-based company who lost a laptop computer valued at $1,100. The loss prompted a flurry of memos and meetings, even though the laptop was an outdated model containing no important documents. "The organization lost 19 people in three months, but no one seemed concerned about that," the vice president points out. "They cared much more about the $1,100 computer. It sent a clear message to all about what the company really values—things over people."

That company seemed to miss an indisputable truth: human talent is a key element of organizational success today. The days when a company's value resided in its access to raw materials or the size of its factories are over. In today's globalized, increasingly service-dominated economy, it is the intellectual capital that provides sustainable competitive advantage. Unfortunately, some companies fail to operate on the basis of this truth. We see this fact play out every day in ways both mundane and perverse.

The talent war is over, and the winner is talent. For a variety of demographic reasons, global organizations are faced with *too few* skilled, qualified workers. A key driver is the aging of the population. This trend will be most dramatic in Europe and Japan. By 2025, the number of people in the critical productivity years of ages 15–64 is projected to fall by 7 percent in Germany, 9 percent in Italy, and 14 percent in Japan, according to *The Economist*. In America, the retirement of baby boomers means that organizations will lose large numbers of experienced workers. RHR International claims that America's 500 largest companies will lose half their senior managers in the next five years. "Unfortunately the next generation of potential leaders has already been decimated by the reengineering and downsizing of the past few decades," *The Economist* reports.

Companies are responding in a variety of ways. Some are depending on a "blended" workforce made up of a mix of core (fixed) and contingent (variable) talent. The challenge is to ensure alignment, at any given time, between the organization's workforce and its strategic goals. Another strategy is to stock up on talent. But this is no panacea, as Enron discovered. Enron recruited strenuously for the best and brightest, hiring up to 250 MBAs a year at the height of its success. It used a "rank and yank" system every year to separate the superstars from the also-rans. Enron rewarded the former with promotions and bonuses. There was no room at Enron for the latter. But stocking up on talent did not protect Enron from going spectacularly wrong.

This discussion is complicated by the fact that the term *talent* is ambiguous. Does the term refer to general competency and aptitude, whether innate or learned? Is it reserved for superstars, those operating at the very tip of the bell curve? Or is it a synonym for the entire workforce? These are questions for another time.

One clear way for organizations to demonstrate their appreciation for their employees is by establishing an equitable balance between the employee's contribution to the organization and the organization's contribution to the employee. The salary an organization pays the employee is a big piece of this equation, but we know it's not as big as many managers may believe. Perhaps the single most important nonmonetary gesture employees want from their organizations is recognition for work well done. "Employees who receive that recognition tend to have higher self-esteem, more confidence, more willingness to take on new challenges, and more eagerness to contribute new ideas and improve productivity," says Donna Deeprose in *How to Recognize and Reward Employees.*

Most companies do a good job of investing in recognition programs around bonuses, formal awards, and the like. I think many of those programs are terrific and necessary, and I discuss several of them in Chapter 9. In institutionalizing employee recognition programs, however, many organizations have lost the immediacy and intimacy of spontaneous recognition gestures. This chapter includes a number of small decencies built around the fundamental goal of appreciating and recognizing individual employees or small teams.

Small decencies by definition are authentic, low cost, spontaneous, and require no elaborate planning or permission, so they are easy to use with frequency. They dovetail quite nicely with recognition expert Bob Nelson's "ASAP Cube" guideline for employee day-to-day recognition. Nelson says that recognition should be:

- *Soon:* Timing is important; don't delay praise.
- *Sincere:* Do it because you're truly appreciative.
- *Specific:* Give details of the achievement.
- *Personal:* Do it in person (or in a handwritten note).
- *Positive:* Don't mix in criticism.
- *Proactive:* Don't wait for perfect performance.

There are endless ways that employee recognition can be provided. The following are informal employee recognition ideas for managers. To be optimal, employee recognition should be designed to fit your workplace culture and the needs and interests of the individuals.

SAY THANK YOU

The easiest employee recognition decency is so obvious, it's frequently overlooked. And that's to say "thank you." It's best to do it one-on-one and in front of peers. Hardly anyone will dispute the value of saying thank you, but in practice many managers become too busy to notice the contributions of others or take the time to articulate appreciation.

The University of Washington surgery residents mentioned in Chapter 4 who sought to learn the names of hospital support staff also challenged each other to say thank you to the often invisible people with the hardest jobs. One such person is Sofia, who cleans the trauma rooms after emergency procedures. As doctors and nurses work to save lives, they quickly discard used dressings, bandages, and surgical cloths on the floor. The practice is an understandable and necessary efficiency, but it also leaves a stomach-churning mess for the custodial staff to deal with after every procedure. The residents work hard to find a moment between emergencies simply to say thank you to Sofia for cleaning up after them. They know their decency has paid off when they hear that other doctors and nurses do the same.

Four Weeks of Thanks

In the workplace, the most effective leaders model the power of individual attention. On this front, there can be no better exemplar than Pat McGovern, the founder and chairman of International Data Group, a $500 million technology publishing and research company.

The 2,600 people who work for McGovern call him "Uncle Pat," for his determination to visit every one of IDG's 65 business units every year and personally chat with as many people as possible. Employees are amazed at his ability to remember names, listen deeply, and act on suggestions. McGovern is all about demonstrating respect for his team, and not just the executives. Everyone at IDG is on McGovern's team. Whether it's the janitor or managing editor, on the occasion of an employee's tenth anniversary with IDG, McGovern invites the employee for a meal at the Ritz-Carlton.

Although IDG publishes hundreds of publications, many people believe that McGovern reads every issue, which is probably impossible as IDG publishes magazines in dozens of languages. Nevertheless, for evidence of this unlikely feat, they point to the hundreds of notes he sends to reporters and columnists every year to congratulate them on their work. Many of these notes are affixed to cubicle walls. McGovern is also known for his generosity, especially at year-end when the chairman goes around the world and personally distributes bonuses. This is no small gesture. To personally thank every IDG employee in the United States alone, more than 1,500 employees, takes almost four weeks. Managers provide him with a list of accomplishments for all their reports, and McGovern memorizes them the night before his visits. He does this because he wants employees to know that he sees them—really sees them—as individuals, and that he considers what they do all day to be meaningful.

The Lost Art of Letter Writing

Thanking people and saying appreciative things about them are good habits to get into. For some reason, it means even more when the thought is delivered in writing. Written thanks can carry more weight, and there's something permanent about gratitude expressed on paper. The note can be filed in a "brag folder," framed, or taken home to share with family.

Ken Iverson, the legendary CEO of Nucor (see Chapter 11) was one of the many leaders who raised the practice of writing notes to subordinates to an art. The note doesn't have to be eloquent, however. It can simply hit the high points of the ASAP cube. Keep a pack of note cards in your desk for convenience.

A more elaborate letter may be appropriate at the end of a substantial project or after an outstanding experience. When was the last time you wrote such a letter to thank an employee or vendor or partner? Think of how valuable such a letter would be, if publicly posted, to the deserving employee as well as his or her colleagues.

I know one executive who made a commitment to write at least one such letter every week. At first he was concerned that each week would not provide an opportunity to write a letter. He was wrong. The more conscious he was about the service he received as he went about his normal day, the more he noticed how often he was delighted by these moments of truth when an employee and customer interact.

I know it's tempting to send off an e-mail instead of taking the time to find a note card and address an envelope, but you know it will mean a lot more if it comes in the mail. Sending an e-mail is better than nothing and allows you to copy supervisors more easily, but to get the full impact of this decency, thanks should be expressed in your own hand on good paper. The recipient will value the sentiment more, and you'll get more out of taking the time to write the letter.

TWO OR THREE WORDS CAN MEAN A LOT

Peggy Noonan, a speechwriter for former President Ronald Reagan, tells a touching story in her memoir, *What I Learned in the Revolution*. Noonan admired Reagan from afar as she wrote speech after speech for him without once setting her eyes on him. Then, four months into her job, President Reagan wrote, "Very good" on a draft of one of the many speeches she had submitted. Noonan was so grateful to receive this compliment that she cut out the words and taped the piece of paper with the president's compliment on her blouse, like a second grader with a star from her favorite teacher.

Here's another idea. When you see someone doing something right, take one of your business cards, write "Great job!" or "Keep up the good work," add the name of the person you are appreciating, sign it, and give him or her the card. That person will have bragging rights for a long time.

A FAMILY AFFAIR

When a manager at W.L. Gore places a positive letter in an associate's personnel file, HR also sends a copy to the associate's home address. It's a small extra effort, but the effort delivers a powerful message. It says that the company acknowledges the associate has a family, that Gore's relationship with the family is important, and that the family adds value to the entire Gore community.

PAYCHECK ENVELOPE PRAISE

The decency discussed here is suitable for smaller offices. Before sealed paycheck envelopes are distributed, write a note on the outside of the envelope expressing your appreciation for the employee's contributions. The more specific you can be, the better. (I understand that this step is not appropriate for large companies with centralized payrolls. But for those offices where checks are still cut manually, it's another way of sharing the credit. By the way, even though many employees elect to have their salary automatically deposited into their checking accounts, they typically still receive an envelope with a receipt at the workplace.)

PRIORITIZE PRAISE

You can call it leader accessibility or "managing by walking around (MBWA)," as Tom Peters phrased it in *In Search of Excellence*. It's about mobility. In fact, at its root, the word *lead* comes from an Old English word that means "go, travel, guide." That means leaders have to get out from behind their desks to break barriers and make themselves accessible. Each day their goal should be to catch employees doing something right so they can praise them. Nothing means as much to a worker as being caught by the boss in the act of doing something great.

Here's the decency: if you see something that does not please you, make a note of it, and save the constructive feedback for another time. Here's what happens if you don't. A friend of mine remembers working in an import company early in her career. The company president practiced a form of MBWA that I do not recommend. Shortly after arriving at the office each morning, he would stride around the office, his knee clicking loudly from an old sports injury. My friend tensed up every time she heard the clicking because experience had taught her that he was more likely to arrive in her office with criticism rather than praise. Instead of bridging the distance between himself and employees, the boss's morning strolls had become a source of stress and even fear.

Former New York City Mayor Ed Koch did it right. He asked a question that he became well known for as he visited various parts of the sprawling city he led. "How am I doing?" was the inevitable question as he met constituents or popped into municipal offices. And because Ed Koch actually listened to the answers, he learned and connected and became a more effective mayor. Koch was elected mayor three times; only one other mayor in New York City history served that long.

LAUNCH A MEETING WITH A LETTER

Remember the decency about sending letters of praise? This is an extension of the same decency. Begin each meeting by reading a letter or e-mail of praise from a customer, partner, or vendor. Typically, such letters are from a customer or vendor who appreciates the worker who delivered the service. Don't have such letters? Ask for them. They almost certainly exist.

WALL OF FAME

Periodically, post letters from customers or partners praising an employee on a special company bulletin board. If the president of the company sends a letter of praise to an employee, consider posting a copy of it on the board as well. Clear it in advance, though, with the employee. Clearing it with the employee is a decency within the decency. Why should such letters languish inside an employee's personnel file?

VALUABLE AUTOGRAPHS

If you're creating a product, find a way to list the names of the team members who made it possible. Apple's Steve Jobs understood the value of this practice. Every member of the team who designed the first Macintosh computer had his or her signature placed on the inside of the computer case. Developers of software applications typically list the names of the development team somewhere inside the software. That no one but the team knows the code to access the list isn't important. What's most important is knowing that the names are there in some form that will outlive the team, the company, and maybe even the developers themselves.

LITTLE THINGS MEAN A LOT

Bring in coffee, donuts, and snacks to share on an unpredictable basis. Or order a pizza or a huge submarine sandwich for a communal lunch. Don't make a big deal of it, but just say it's a token of how much you appreciate how hard everyone is working. Take care that you don't make a routine of it. Preserve the spontaneity, or else decencies tend to become entitlements. That's not necessarily bad; the organization will benefit from many such transformations. In fact, if the small decency is really effective, it's very difficult to preserve as a small decency. It becomes woven into the fabric of the culture, often has a budget, and is suddenly a big decency. Nevertheless, it's often worth the effort because, as we've seen, small decencies are powerful.

Here's another example: Sam Colin, founder of Colin Service Systems janitorial services in White Plains, New York, had a practice of handing out rolls of Life Savers candy to employees he wanted to appreciate.

EXECUTIVE COFFEE CART

Cigna Group, an insurance company headquartered in Hartford, Connecticut, has an executive coffee cart. But this is not a cart that goes around the executive suite to serve the managers. During the busiest times of the year, Cigna executives personally push coffee carts around the office, serving drinks and refreshments to their colleagues. As they serve, executives coach and encourage their colleagues, as well as hear about real consumer issues from those who know customer concerns the best.

INVITE AN EMPLOYEE TO REPRESENT YOU AT MEETINGS

How many meetings, seminars, and conferences both inside the company and outside the company would it be worthwhile for you to attend? Probably more than your schedule can accommodate. Why not invite select subordinates to go in your place and represent you? If you select carefully, the employee will get a psychic kick out of representing you, getting off-site, meeting new people, and learning new things. This form of recognition is especially convenient if the meetings are in-house or local. If the meetings involve travel or significant out-of-pocket expense, the gesture is no longer a small decency, but one worth considering just the same. At an appropriate point, the employee can share some of what is learned with team members. You will benefit by being known as someone who values the work of other groups so much that you will send a representative when you cannot attend.

THE GIFT OF TIME

Depending on the limits of your authority and the culture of the company, you may be able to offer time off to reward an employee for exceptional service or long hours. As a small decency, the offer has to be outside of vacation or personal day policies and you have to know that you have the authority to manage personally the employee's schedule. Options may include:

- Day off
- Work-at-home day
- Three-hour lunch break
- Late arrival or early departure

One vice president at Johnson & Johnson could feel the stress building in everyone—including himself—as the holidays approached. His department had been working hard on a major

initiative, and everyone seemed behind in their holiday prepara-
tions. At a department meeting, he told everyone to take half a
day off sometime in the next few weeks. It didn't count as vacation, and people didn't need to clear the time with him. They
simply needed to make sure a colleague could cover for them if
an emergency came up while they were off shopping or baking
cookies. As one mother of two young children said, "I was able
to shop on a Wednesday afternoon. There were no crowds, and
I didn't have the kids in tow, so I did more in four hours than I
would have in eight on a weekend. It was the best gift ever from
a boss. I felt so much more in control for the rest of the season."

FREEDOM TO CHOOSE

Another no-cost way to recognize employees who have done a
good job is to let them pick their next project or swap a task with
someone else. For instance, if one person has completed a project involving significant travel, it would be nice to offer him or
her the option of a project with no travel. If a salesperson has
been doing a great job standing at the front of the trade show
booth greeting customers, she (and her feet!) may appreciate
swapping with the person sitting behind the order desk.

THINK CREATIVELY

After a few years in the labor relations department at Tenneco, I
moved to corporate headquarters where I became director of
employee relations. One of my better decisions was to hire Mike
Fadden as a compensation manager. Mike was a genius at compensation creativity. Here's an example of what I mean.

It was a time when business was flat. The word had come down from the corner office that raises would be limited to a 2 percent cost-of-living increase. I knew this news would upset many employees. I was especially frustrated because there were a handful of employees who had so spectacularly gone beyond expectations that they merited a more respectable raise. But what could I do? Then Mike came to the rescue. "Don't wait. Give these special few the cost-of-living increase one month early."

There was no rule against it, so that's what I did. The employees appreciated it beyond the monetary value of the gesture. Even though the actual extra money was trivial, the gesture of giving it early made a huge difference. My takeaway: even when your hands are tied, you can always find a way to make a memory.

Other managers use their artistic skills to reward top performers. The *Wall Street Journal* published a story about Sandy Schroeder, a market coach for Taco Bell, who makes commemorative plaques for high performers at the 36 restaurants she oversees in Indiana. Schroeder starts with music CDs. Then she paints each with the recipient's name, the date, and such tags as, "Performance Is a Smash Hit" and "You Rock!" A plaque takes around 40 minutes to make and costs about $5, she says, adding that most recipients display them in their store offices.

Many leaders invoke the Golden Rule when designing employee recognition programs. "Do unto others as you would have others do unto you" is a valuable guideline in life, but when it comes to appreciating employees, I suggest applying the Platinum Rule: Do unto others as they would have you do unto them.

Many creative and simple ways of appreciating others may be found in the *Life's Little Instruction Book* series by H. Jackson Brown, Jr. Here are just a few:

- Compliment three people every day.
- Rebuild a broken relationship.
- Become the most positive and enthusiastic person you know.
- Keep secrets no matter what.
- Give people more than they expect and do it cheerfully.
- Earn your success based on service to others, not at the expense of others.
- Compliment publicly; criticize privately.

Here are some other ideas for tangible decencies that might appeal to recipients. The key is to keep the ideas spontaneous, authentic to you, and meaningful to the recipient.

- "Welcome to the team" flowers on the first day of work.
- Brown-bag welcoming lunch to meet new employees.
- Post a sign at the entry with the new employee's name.
- Display employee awards and certificates on the company's Hall of Fame wall or Web site.
- Give movie tickets for a job well done.
- Write a letter to the spouse of an employee to thank him or her for the support enabling the employee to do his or her best.
- On the day a new employee starts work, send flowers or another appropriate token to the spouse or partner of the employee.
- Give out $2 bills as symbols of instant recognition. Yes, they still exist, and in the United States $2 bills hold an extraordinary fascination. For some reason, a crisp $2 bill has much more than twice the impact of a $1 bill. For an even bigger impact, sign the bill. Watch the employee pin it up in his or her workspace as a reminder of your gesture.

- Relieve workplace stress by celebrating holidays not usually celebrated such as Groundhog Day, Arbor Day, Bastille Day, Polish Independence Day, and summer solstice.
- Recognize improvement, not just top performers.
- Make business cards listing employee accomplishments.

The most important form of recognition is simply noticing the work. At the end of the day, all these gestures are important. But the gestures are memorable only to the extent they signal what is truly critical: that you, the leader, recognize and appreciate the individual contributions of people who look to you for leadership.

6

Listening Decencies

Courage is what it takes to stand up and speak.
Courage is also what it takes to sit down and listen.

WINSTON CHURCHILL

Mergers and acquisitions are a challenging and an increasingly important fact of business life. Virtually all mergers and acquisitions of publicly traded companies are justified on the basis of promised strategic synergies and cost savings. The value of the merged businesses is always said to be greater than the sum of the parts. The reality is that for some stakeholders, the value is less. As for cost savings, those may be real, but the costs in human terms can be substantial.

Mergers and acquisitions are a challenge because it is very difficult to mesh two distinct corporate cultures into one. The difficulty is further compounded by the frequent reality that the cultures to be meshed tomorrow into a streamlined team were just yesterday bitter competitors. Addressing the culture factor requires extensive planning, communicating, credible expectation setting, and sensitivity. Underlying all these tools is the decency of listening—really listening—to people on both sides of the transaction.

This lesson hit close to home for me in 1988. On the first day of April of that year, the privately held Lee Hecht Harrison outplacement firm was acquired by Adecco, the world's largest staffing company. The off again/on again negotiations lasted over seven months. The "off again" pauses had little to do with the financial terms of the deal. It had everything to do with the sensitivity and anxiety of the three LHH partners as we tried to protect the culture that we had constructed over many years. The key negotiator on Adecco's side was its mergers and acquisitions (M&A) director, John Hamachek. John was focused, intense, and financially brilliant, with a strong sense of integrity. Neither small talk nor a conspicuous sense of humor pervaded his negotiating style.

My partners and I were concerned about a number of cultural issues that had nothing to do with the financial terms. Bob Lee, Bob Hecht, and I set to work identifying all of our nonfinancial concerns about the upcoming acquisition. Then I called John and told him we had some issues. Could he visit us and leave his calculator behind?

John surprised us with his immediate willingness to come and sit with us. I booked a conference room at a nearby hotel for two days, fully anticipating that we would need at least that much time to assuage our anxieties and concerns. The meeting started at 9 a.m. and lasted through lunch. To the surprise of the three of us, this tough negotiator had suddenly morphed into a genuinely concerned, open, and sensitive partner who demonstrated his eagerness to understand what we had to say. John had his notebook out. He leaned forward and made eye contact. He never interrupted. Such was his capacity for empathy that he even raised important issues that we ourselves had not anticipated.

By the time lunch rolled around, my partners and I had run out of questions and issues. We were more than satisfied as we thanked John for his willingness to put our minds at ease. Our concerns about culture fit, personal career issues, autonomy, and job security for our people had been more than relieved. We renewed our commitment to move forward with the acquisition.

The day after the acquisition was announced, the chief executive of Adecco USA, said he was coming to New York to meet with me and my direct reports. My first reaction was one of anxiety and suspicion. Despite the reassuring time with John Hamachek, I anticipated that the honeymoon would be ending early and that we would get our marching orders from headquarters.

On the appointed date, the CEO scheduled a full-day offsite at the Yale Club. My executive committee and I met him in a small conference room at the famous facility. He greeted us and then personally arranged the chairs in a tight semicircle and placed himself at the center. He then invited us to make ourselves comfortable and to ask him anything—literally anything we wanted to know about the company, its management, strategies, and rationale for the acquisition. He also invited us to ask questions about him personally. He said he wanted to hear about our lives, our families, our interests, our hopes, and our concerns. As the questions unfolded, I marveled that there was virtually no talk of market share, budgets, and policies. Instead we talked about our industry and why we chose it and how we could work together as a team to make our experience more meaningful.

That day we observed Adecco honoring the only promise we asked of the new company: to be our strategic partner, not just our corporate boss. The relationship is in its nineteenth year, all of them productive. I believe the merger has worked partly because Adecco made the time to listen to us at these initial meetings, which left an enduring memory of an early decency.

Listening is the essence of effective meetings and interpersonal encounters of all varieties: one-on-one, group, and telephone conversations. Listening means more than gathering and making sense of information. Listening, and more critically, *noticeably* listening, is a signal of respect. Anyone can improve his or her level of performance by thinking strategically about listening and practicing effective listening skills.

We all appreciate the benefits of quality listening. Next to physical survival, the greatest need of a human being is psychological survival—to be understood, to be affirmed, to be validated, and to be appreciated. Don't we identify the best moments in business when we see evidence that we have been truly heard? We have been listening to others all our lives, so we can be forgiven for assuming that we already know how to listen. Actually, many of us pay little attention to the quality of our listening. Especially in business situations, we are too distracted or too busy planning what we are going to say next or thinking about the bigger picture or possible implications of situations to truly attend to what someone else is saying.

Here are a number of listening decencies. Many of these might seem obvious, but they all contribute to a sense that you are either truly listening or being truly listened to.

DON'T ASSUME YOU SHOULD TALK MORE

The decent—and effective—thing to do is to talk less. Whether you are conversing with a customer, problem solving with a colleague, or negotiating with a vendor, it rarely follows that your goals will be best served by your talking more. In fact, listening is by far the more powerful approach in each of these cases.

APPLY THE 60-SECOND RULE

In a one-on-one conversation, most people can't really listen for more than 60 seconds. Yes, what you have to say is important. No, you can't do your subject justice in 60 seconds. That's fine. The 60-second rule says that you should divide your subject into thoughts that can be expressed in 60 seconds or less. If someone is interested in what you say during the first 60 seconds, he or she will ask a question, and then you can continue for another 60 seconds, and so on. Now you have a conversation instead of a lecture or monologue.

RESIST THE TEMPTATION TO INTERRUPT

Short of announcing a fire, it is never good to interrupt someone talking to you. That includes interrupting people even if it's to agree with them. Wait until people finish making their points before you speak. Don't jump in with your own suggestions before they explain what they have already done, plan to do, or have thought about doing.

If you occupy a position of greater authority or prestige, any interruption will be seen as a sign of you asserting your power. If you do so, you eliminate many of the benefits of listening. In the worst cases, people may even withhold important information from you. The best way to guarantee this counterproductive outcome is to perfect any of the following listening indecencies:

- Criticizing them for getting into their situation
- Making judgmental faces or sounds
- "Fixing" their problem with a quick suggestion
- Interrogating them to make them come to a predetermined conclusion
- Trying to cheer them up by telling them things aren't so bad

VALUE SILENCE

Respecting silence in conversations is a decency. Some people need to take significant conversational pauses to reflect and put their thinking into words. That doesn't make them slow or dim-witted; to the contrary, their comfort with silence may be a marker of intelligence.

There is an executive I respect for his reflective style. Let's call him Bill. Everyone eventually describes Bill as wise, sage, or insightful. The operative word is "eventually." I noticed that many colleagues were often too impatient to get the best out of this executive. For to get the best out of Bill, one had to tolerate a bit of silence as he reflected. Unfortunately, for many executives even five seconds of silence is interminable. I noticed that people in meetings with Bill filled his pauses with questions, comments, jokes—anything to avoid the dreaded silence. When a new MBA joined his department, he was so desperate to make his mark that he used Bill's pauses as an opening to give his opinions. Within months, though, he figured out that if he was silent through these pauses, he would learn a lot more.

SEEK TO UNDERSTAND BEFORE
SEEKING TO BE UNDERSTOOD

This is the fifth of Stephen Covey's *Seven Habits of Highly Successful People*. It's difficult to overestimate the importance of seeking to understand before seeking to be understood. This habit is the basis of authentic relationships and is a powerful listening decency that disarms antagonists and makes allies of people around you. It may be the most powerful learning technique available because it leverages on your circle of influence. Why? Because before you seek to influence others, you yourself must be influenceable.

AVOID ASKING QUESTIONS TO WHICH
YOU ALREADY HAVE THE ANSWER

Sometimes we make statements with a question mark at the end. These are not real questions, but are our opinions or decisions masquerading as questions. I'm talking about "questions" such as, "Do you think we should consider outsourcing?" when you've already decided that outsourcing is the way to go. These "questions" are not going to fool anybody. They are disrespectful and ineffective. If you have an agenda—if you believe outsourcing is the way to go—it's much better to simply state your position up front. There is nothing wrong with having an agenda. The problem is trying to disguise the agenda by asking questions that you hope will get people to arrive at your predetermined conclusion. When you've got an answer, maybe it's time to find better questions.

I hasten to add that I'm speaking of situations in which you want the candid opinions of others. In other cases, it's vital that you know the answers to the questions you ask. Attorneys conducting a deposition or cross-examination are well advised to ask only questions to which they know the answer.

OPEN NOTEBOOK, OPEN MIND

Have you ever noticed that some people go into meetings carrying a notebook or notepad but that they never open it? When I see that, I think, "Closed notebook, closed mind." They are signaling that they are not there to learn or have a dialogue.

So when you go to a meeting or when you go to a colleague's office to get an opinion about a project or work matter, here's a subtle decency that will make all the difference. Go in with a notebook. Open it. If you're one-on-one with somebody, request permission to take notes. Then listen. And then make a note or two . . . or three. Not as an FBI agent, but as a learner, a partner in inquiry. And then read the note and ask if what you recorded is what the colleague meant to say. Rare is the conversation that does not result in at least one interesting thought. Write it down. Make it clear by your body language that you are in this for your education and the organization's welfare. Your colleagues will be hoping that you come by.

HAVE A DECENT CONVERSATION CLOSE

There are lots of ways to close a conversation, but for my money, there is nothing more decent than, "Is there anything else I can help you with?" or "Is there anything else I can do for you?" The answer gives you one last opportunity to listen to what people have to say in answer to an open-ended, altruistic question.

Frequently, the last comments are the most memorable because they are the last thing the parties hear. Let the other party have the last word.

THERE IS A TIME FOR MULTITASKING

"To do two things at once is to do neither," Publius declared in his seventh maxim, circa 42 BC. You might think you can listen to someone and check your e-mail at the same time. But, trust me, you can't. Listening is a full-time job.

What? You really can listen to others while you multitask? All right, I believe you. I still say, don't do it. The perception that you are not giving someone your full attention will negate whatever efficiency you hope to achieve. People are exquisitely tuned in to any sign of disrespect. People notice when you don't listen to them attentively. Simply stated, it is a decency for you to give people your full attention, and they will rightfully resent it when you agree to do so and then don't.

We live in a complex world of time compression where speed is a competitive advantage. The ability to multitask can be necessary. I don't deny that. It's all about timing and choices. Tidy your desk while you are on hold. Read the latest trade magazine while you are on the treadmill. But don't do anything but listen when someone is talking to you.

NO ADVICE

A lot of people come to me for business advice. My inclination is to ask questions before I answer them. I ask them to tell me more about their situation; I offer to point out options or complications they may not have considered. But I try not to offer advice in the sense of telling other people, "This is what you should do." Advice can be disempowering.

When someone asks you for advice, they really do want something important from you, and it might not be your recommendations about what they might do. What they usually want is a little space so they can think out loud while they figure out what's important to them. In support of that process, ask questions: "What other options have you considered?" Reflect feelings: "You seem frightened." Challenge assumptions: "When did you first come to believe that . . . ?" Remind them that they are in the best position to make decisions.

If they ask for information you have, give it to them or, better yet, point out where they can find it. Find a way to suggest options they may not have considered or consequences they may not have foreseen. Most of all, offer them your undivided attention so they can think out loud in the presence of someone they trust. Listen. You will be surprised how often they come to a good decision. Moreover, a decision that is owned in this way has a better chance of being implemented successfully.

"I WONDER . . . "

One of the smartest and most decent ways to get someone talking so that you can listen is using the words, "I wonder . . . " In his book *Plain Talk*, Nucor CEO Ken Iverson describes how this phrase may be applied by a middle manager to tweak an organization's compensation system, perhaps the most change-resistant process in any corporation:

- "I wonder if we couldn't find ways to get a little more motivation and productivity in return for our compensation dollars."
- "I wonder how many people here feel truly challenged and inspired, day in and day out, by the earning opportunities we currently offer them."
- "I wonder how close a connection employees see between how hard they work each day and what we pay them for their work."
- "I wonder if we couldn't find tangible productivity measures for groups of people where no such measures are applicable for individuals."
- "I wonder if our approach to compensation might be falling a step or two behind the changes we're trying to make . . . Is it doing all it could to advance our initiatives on teamwork, innovation, and cycle time reduction."

When you start a conversation by saying "I wonder . . . " you encourage people to participate with you in a topic that ideally is of interest to them as well. By approaching the topic in this fashion, you signal an open mind that welcomes reflective comments and fragments of solutions. The expectation is that responses to "I wonder . . ." phrases will not be ruthlessly evaluated.

Let me be very clear about something. Decency requires that people who ask the "I wonder . . ." phrase genuinely be open to wonder. They can't have their minds made up before asking. This formula provides the opening for their ideas, not for yours.

EXECUTIVE LISTENING

Iverson's "I wonder . . ." gesture is a listening device that, like the others in this chapter, can be used by anyone at any level and in a variety of settings. As we move up the corporate hierarchy, listening often becomes more difficult. Executives always have more demands on their time, more direct reports, and bigger issues. Power often creates obstructions to listening opportunities. Executives at the top of organizations not only have to practice the skills and decencies covered in this chapter, but they also have to adjust their attitudes and consciously make themselves available to listen. The next chapter addresses decencies that allow us to be accessible and approachable executives.

7

Executive Humility Decencies

*It is far more impressive when others
discover your good qualities without your help.*

AUTHOR UNKNOWN

In 1971, I was in my seventh year of corporate life, employed by a division of Houston-based Tenneco, Inc., one of the up-and-coming energy companies of the time. The business concentrated on oil, gas transmission, petrochemicals, and plastics. The company also owned the Newport News Shipyard, which built the biggest aircraft carriers and submarines in the world. It owned thousands of acres of land in Kern County, California, where almonds and raisins were produced.

Tenneco was a reflection of Texas. It was big. Everything was oversized, from the offices to the restrooms. The executives were big-boned Texans, one taller than the other. The CEO was straight out of central casting, a tall, slender, silver-haired executive. He was polished, elegant—the model of executive bearing.

As a division-level manager, I was surprised, but delighted, to be asked to attend the three-day Tenneco conference at Columbia Lakes, Tenneco's Texas-sized suburban-Houston conference center. Two hundred and fifty of us were ushered into the auditorium for the keynote presentation by the CEO. David Ellis's speech had been billed as an early peek at Tenneco's five-year strategy.

Less than five minutes into the talk, Ellis looked up from his notes, took a long pause, then closed his folder, and said, "I don't want to talk about Tenneco's strategy. I want to talk about something more important. I want to talk about executive pomposity. No strategic plan will be achieved at a company that reeks of executive pomposity."

Ellis told us about the time he phoned the Tenneco vice president of compensation and benefits, only to be screened by a well-meaning assistant. "May I say what the call is about?" she asked. Ellis identified himself as the CEO and asked the assistant if her boss was in his office. The answer was yes. Ellis asked if he was on the phone or in a meeting. The answer was neither. Ellis then instructed the assistant to hold the phone. He then walked out of his corner office, took the stairs one floor down to the VP's area.

The assistant was still holding the phone, ashen-faced, as Ellis walked in. He smiled at the assistant to show he was not angry at her. Without knocking, he walked into the VP's office. "Okay, you're here! Your telephone is going to ring in three minutes. It'll be me." Then Ellis turned on his heel and walked back to his office.

When the phone rang, the VP immediately answered it. "Good, you picked up your own phone. That's more like it." Ellis told us that he then asked the VP to consider the adverse impact of productivity associated with executives having calls routinely screened.

This was the first time I'd heard the term "executive pomposity," and the words have been etched in my mind ever since.

Many leaders let their authority go to their heads. It breeds a sense of entitlement. All this attitude does is distance these executives from their colleagues and customers, and, ultimately, from their business. As much as it might inflate their egos, pomposity deflates others around them.

Pomposities can take on a life of their own. Bethlehem Steel was losing market share in the 1970s, reports John Strohmeyer in his book *Crisis in Bethlehem*, but that didn't stop the ailing steel behemoth's executives from building themselves an executive golf course. When the middle managers began complaining, the executives wasted no time in addressing the complaint. They built a *second* golf course for middle managers. After predictable criticism from the union and workers, the executives built a third golf course for rank and file employees. This was during the time when the U.S. steel industry was losing market share and shedding jobs. "Imagine building *three* golf courses just to remind everyone where they fall in the corporate hierarchy!" bristled Nucor's Ken Iverson (italics his). "What does that say about a company's values and corporate culture?"

There is nothing inevitable about executive privilege and executive pomposity. One does not necessarily have to follow the other. Chapter 11 features five executives who disdain every instance of executive pomposity and are no less effective leaders for it. They recognize that pomposity is counterproductive in today's flattened organizations.

TELEPHONE DECENCIES

Since I introduced the idea of executive pomposity with Ellis's story about screening calls, I'll continue to talk more about how executives can demonstrate approachability and respect for others through telephone practices.

Unless I'm on another phone conversation or meeting with someone, I always personally answer my direct calls. Is it an occasional wrong number or pushy salesperson? Sure. But as a clear commitment to reducing pomposity, there's nothing like it. Not surprisingly, once the word gets around that this is your practice, people become more judicious around their decision to have their calls screened. And as for the message to callers, it's this: I consider your call very important, and I don't want to waste your time dealing with an intermediary. On the other hand, I want you to respect my time. That means identify yourself immediately, get to the point, and if I say I'm not interested, respect my decision.

It's all about reputation. People talk, and word spreads. Answering your own calls is not without cost, but it remains a simple gesture that reinforces a commitment to an open, confident, decent culture.

HOSTS AND GUESTS

In any social interaction—and work is a crucible of social interactions—it's critical to be aware if you are operating as a host or a guest. There are expectations with each role, and woe to the manager who fails to understand the distinction. There are real differences between the social rules that apply outside the office and in the office, but the rules are frequently blurred and confused. Many of the interpersonal conflicts at work can be traced to confusion about host/guest obligations.

In many cases, managers act as hosts. When you convene a meeting, you are acting as a host. And if you are a host, the people participating at the meeting are your guests. On some level, they expect to be treated as guests. This is true even for meetings at which attendance is mandatory. The duties of a host, at work and elsewhere, are to make guests feel welcome. If attendance at the meeting requires guests to dig into their pockets, it is the duty of the host to reimburse them.

Of course, guests at the office have responsibilities too. The first duty of a guest is to respond promptly to the invitation. Other responsibilities are to show up on time, dress appropriately, and participate fully.

After graduate school and then the army, I became a labor relations manager for a division of Tenneco operating largely in the coal regions of Pennsylvania. The first several years of my work life revolved around hundreds of meetings with labor unions—grievance meetings, arbitrations, negotiations, and meetings to resolve wildcat strikes. Given that the meetings involved squabbling parties in an adversarial process, the meetings were more or less acrimonious. But at least the meetings were long and drawn-out.

In the 1960s, northeast Pennsylvania had more than its share of frustrated, demanding, and often angry union members. The world they knew was coming to an end. Coal mines were closing down. Unemployment in the industry was well over 20 percent. Many wives had to become primary wage earners in local textile factories, adding to the humiliation of proud former mine workers.

The first real meeting I organized on my own was a union grievance meeting. I arrived a few minutes late, to find six or seven beefy guys, members of Local 401 of the International Brotherhood of Teamsters, seated at the table looking very unfriendly. Most of the men smoked cheap, really nasty cigars. Fortunately, I wasn't offered one. The guys (they were all guys) were clearly tired and sweaty from the long day of driving 18-wheelers to and from New York and Philadelphia. The biggest and beefiest of the group was Leo, their local union business agent.

We debated and hassled over their issues for at least two hours. Eventually, I had a check mark by all the agenda items. When it was clear to me that all the agenda items had been covered, I thanked the members of the grievance committee, closed my books, and got up to leave.

"Where the hell do you think you're going?" Leo said.

"Well," I mumbled, "our meeting is over. We've covered all the items on the agenda."

Leo wasn't listening to my excuse. "Are you walking out on us?" he shouted.

"Not really," I said, as I put my briefcase down and slumped back in my chair.

"Of course you are! Looks like all you learned in that fancy college you went to was Insulting People 101."

I later realized that Leo was mostly giving a new kid a hard time, but there was a durable lesson embedded in all that bluster. I learned something that April day in 1964 that I have never forgotten. From that moment forward, I've made it my business that for any meeting that I call, I will be the first to sit down and the last one to get up to leave. I've decided that this practice is a subtle signal of humility and respect—a small decency as powerful as a handshake. Being a true host at meetings I call demonstrates that I don't think more of myself than of those I invited.

ADJUST THE ENVIRONMENT

Thirty years later, I learned a different lesson about meeting dynamics from Ray. Lee Hecht Harrison was in intense competition with two other human resources companies for the acquisition of a desirable New Jersey–based outplacement firm. Ray was in charge of getting the deal done. The target firm's owner decided it was time to disclose to his management team the fact that acquisition discussions were under way. So he called a meeting with us and his key people. The purpose of the meeting was to address their understandable concerns.

When we walked in, we could immediately tell that the atmosphere was tense and that the attendees were very anxious. There were seven coworkers, and they all sat on one side of a long conference table, leaving empty seats on the opposite side for the three of us. After the introductions and some opening remarks by the owner of the firm, Ray interrupted and asked, "May I suggest a different seating arrangement? If this deal materializes, we will be working very closely together as one integrated team. So why don't we start to see how that feels by intermingling with each other right now?" With that, he led the reshuffling of the seating so that it was no longer an us-versus-them configuration.

Two months later the acquisition was consummated. We subsequently learned that the three offering prices were very close. We also learned that we had not, in fact, submitted the absolute highest offer. Nevertheless, the offer the company accepted was ours. What tipped the balance in our favor in the eyes of the smaller outplacement firm was the gesture about seating that Ray led, and the powerful, inclusive symbolism it represented. In the ensuing years, I've used this approach many times, and, more importantly, I have attended meetings that my colleagues have scheduled where they did the same thing. It always has the effect of reducing us-them issues, while increasing collaboration and a sense of, "We're all in this thing together." Rearranging seating is a small decency that allows a leader to be with, not removed from, the working team, favors integration over separation, and helps create a win-win outcome.

TAKE AN EMPLOYEE'S JOB FOR A DAY

It was just before Christmas, and the bank lobby in Chicago was busy with holiday shoppers. Many shoppers stared in curiosity at the sight of a line of tellers, all middle-aged men in suits. It turns out that the managers had given the regular tellers the day off and had made it possible by taking the tellers' jobs for the day. You don't have to wait for Christmas. Nor do you have to make it a big departmental program. If you value an employee and can reasonably do his or her job, give that employee the day off and take over.

Some vice presidents have worked shifts as receptionists. Actually, there are multiple benefits to be gained from this practice, above and beyond the recognition of individual employees. How do you think employees feel about a company when they see the vice president volunteering to be the receptionist for a day?

We know that there are also benefits to managers knowing how to do certain jobs. Some companies even expect this type of cross-training. Before Charles Schwab promotes someone to be branch manager, he or she must have had hands-on experience in virtually every aspect of the business, from taking orders at a call center to welcoming customers at the retail level. PepsiCo requires new

MBAs to manage fast-food restaurants, sometimes in the toughest neighborhoods, before taking up positions in strategy development, marketing, or finance. If you keep the practice informal, low key, and spontaneous, you'll demonstrate that you are not above others and you'll also demonstrate a higher level of decency.

SHARE THE CREDIT, HOARD THE BLAME

When things go well, share the credit. When things go badly, be known as someone who is accountable. There will be time to sort out the problem and learn from it. But be known as someone whose first instinct is to fix the problem rather than fix the blame. Chapter 11 profiles five executives who elevate small decencies to an art form. They are all masters at giving credit to people other than themselves.

IT'S OKAY TO DISPLAY DOUBT WHEN YOU'RE IN DOUBT

On occasion and when it's authentic, it's okay for a leader to say he or she doesn't know. Great decisions begin with great people who have the courage to say, "I don't know." The conventional wisdom suggests that any leader who does not project absolute certainty in his or her decisions or convictions is doomed. Actually, leadership demands a dynamic balance of certainty and doubt. When you don't know, say so.

In *The Seven Habits of Highly Effective People*, Stephen Covey tells a story illustrating that certainty in leaders is not always a virtue. Two battleships were at sea on maneuvers in heavy weather. The captain of the lead battleship was on watch as night fell. The ships were traveling through patchy fog that made visibility poor. Then the lookout on the wing of the bridge reported, "Light, bearing on the starboard bow."

"Is it steady or moving astern?" the captain called out.

"Steady, Captain," came the answer, confirming that they were on a dangerous course.

The captain called to the signalman, "Signal that ship, tell them: We are on a collision course, advise you change course 20 degrees."

"Advise you change course 20 degrees," came the reply.

The captain said. "Send this message: 'I am a captain. You change course 20 degrees.'"

"I'm a seaman second class," was the reply. "Advise you change course 20 degrees."

Now furious, the captain spat out, "Send this message: 'Change course 20 degrees. I'm a battleship.'"

Back came word from the flashing light, "I'm a lighthouse."

MAKE YOURSELF ACCESSIBLE

Humility is the opposite of pomposity, and part of humility is knowing that you don't have all the answers. Those around you have good ideas, too, but you have to find a way to be accessible to others at all levels of the company so that you can hear the ideas. Humility is also a bridge to collaboration, another important leadership characteristic. Here are some ways that different leaders and companies model humility and the importance of collaboration.

Monthly Birthday Breakfast

Cisco Systems CEO John Chambers is concerned about keeping lines of communication open between himself and Cisco's employees. So for the past 10 years Chambers hosted a monthly hour-long birthday breakfast. Any Cisco employee who has a birthday in that month gets to come and ask the CEO anything. To make the dialogue as candid as possible, no directors or VPs are allowed. "It's how I keep my finger on the pulse of what's working and what's not," Chambers says.

Standing Lunch Date

Announce that on a regular day and time and at a specified place—say in the company cafeteria every Thursday at noon— you will have an open lunch table to which all are welcome. John Kador, president of the Geneva, Illinois, Rotary Club, tried this strategy to make new members feel welcome, build teamwork, and move projects forward. He announced he would be at a local eatery at noon every Thursday. Sometimes six or seven Rotarians joined Kador, and sometimes it was just one or two. And did it ever happen that no one showed up? That happened a few times, Kador acknowledged, but he never regarded it as a setback. "How often do I have an uninterrupted hour thinking about work that is important to me," he said.

Invite a Colleague to Lunch

In today's world, many businesspeople have gone from the extreme of the three-martini lunch to no lunch at all. Many people eat at their desks or skip lunch altogether. In dismissing lunch, we miss an important opportunity to connect on an informal level with our coworkers. Schedules will vary for different organizations, but I believe that a well-thought-out lunch practice is a decency that can go a long way to demonstrating your desire to spend time with others in the company. It's a good way to informally communicate some information about the company's goals or values. And if you listen, you can learn something too.

Open Office Hours

At Genentech, number one on *Fortune*'s Best Companies to Work For in 2006, every member of the leadership team is available for "office hours" once a month. The decency of having regular office hours is really just a variation of the open-door policy. It requires no more than having individuals agreeing to be in their office for one hour per month, with the door open, and having no other agenda than to be of service to whoever shows up.

If you try this idea, all I ask is that you clear your desk and wait. Shut off your computer monitor. Have someone else take your phone calls. People are very sensitive. If they feel they will interrupt you, they will stay away. If you want people to show up, you have to show up first.

FACE YOUR PROBLEMS OR CRITICS HEAD-ON

Do you remember the movie *The Hunt for Red October*? There's a scene in the movie that reminds me that sometimes the best way to confront problems and critics is to move toward them, not away from them. Captain Marko Ramius, the USSR's best submarine skipper, sees on the sonar screen that a torpedo fired by a U.S. submarine is quickly heading toward the Russian sub. Instead of trying to evade the torpedo, Captain Ramius orders *Red October* to come about and race directly toward the threatening torpedo. The Russian skipper understood something critical about torpedoes. When fired, they are armed to explode after a certain distance. By racing toward the torpedo, the captain changed the target distance and disrupted the torpedo's programming. It bounced harmlessly off the Russian sub. Instead of running away from the problem, he moved closer to it and in the process disarmed it.

The same truth applies to any relationship on or off the job. As a leader, don't avoid those who have different perspectives; reach out and bring them closer. If you sense someone has an issue with you, don't wait till it explodes. Seek them out and ask them about it. Such conversations are way too rare in today's business environment.

THE BUSINESS OF APOLOGY

Apologies are serious business. New evidence demonstrates that the magic healing power of the two words "I'm sorry" can go a long way to mediating office disputes, avoiding litigation, and minimizing legal damage awards. If you want to minimize liability, the best thing to do is to keep your mistakes small. But if you make a big one, there is still something you can do to minimize liability. Just say you're sorry. Saying you're sorry effectively is one of the most powerful small decencies available to any leader. It involves two words and only seconds of your time. Far from diminishing your importance, an apology demonstrates humility, respect for others, and a desire to learn, all of which are traits of strong leaders. Refusing to apologize after having made a mistake demonstrates pomposity of the worst kind.

Believe it or not, some doctors are learning that an apology can be good medicine. An apology often prevents malpractice claims. The Veterans Affairs Medical Center in Lexington, Kentucky, has proved that the rage that arises out of the injury and fuels so much of the animus is almost always drained away by a sincere apology. Since 1998, this VA center has had a policy of admitting medical errors, apologizing for them, and initiating a claim—even when the family itself has no idea that medical error contributed to a patient's death. Skeptics predicted that "extreme honesty" would be a liability nightmare. But legal costs at the hospital are now among the lowest in the VA system. An honest apology relieves suspicion and a sense of hurt in the hearts of malpractice victims and their families.

People often hesitate to apologize because they equate the words "I'm sorry" with a guilty plea. Apology involves risks; but so does refusing to apologize. More and more jurisdictions are passing legislation to allow individuals and corporations to offer a sincere apology as part of their dispute resolution process without fear of legal liability. Two new studies by a researcher at the University of Missouri-Columbia found that an apology averts lawsuits and helps promote settlements.

"Several factors, such as the nature of the apology, the severity of the injury, and other evidence of responsibility, affect the capacity of an apology to facilitate settlement," said Jennifer Robbennolt, a scholar in the area of psychology and law, torts, and dispute resolution. She is currently on the faculty at the University of Illinois. Professor Robbennolt conducted the cited study while she was a senior fellow in the Center for the Study of Dispute Resolution at the University of Missouri-Columbia School of Law. "Policymakers and litigants must take into account these complex issues when making decisions about the appropriate role of apologies in settling civil disputes," she wrote in an article published in the *Michigan Law Review*.

In the two studies, participants read a scenario describing a pedestrian-bicycle accident. They were asked to take on the role of the injured person and evaluate a settlement offer from the other party, based on information about the injuries, the other party's conduct, and each party's responsibility for causing the accident.

Robbennolt found that when a full apology was given, 73 percent of the respondents would accept the settlement offer. When no apology was given, 52 percent would accept, but when a partial apology was given, only 35 percent would accept. "An offender who offered a full apology was seen as experiencing more regret, as being more moral and more likely to be careful in the future than one offering a partial or no apology," Robbennolt explains.

Because of studies like these, California, Texas, and Massachusetts have recently passed "expressions of sympathy" statutes. These are laws that are intended to make it easier to apologize without liability attaching itself to the statement. Many companies now recognize the redeeming character of a good apology—not least because victims and juries often accept it as grounds for reducing any damage award.

For instance, the Toro Company, a Minnesota manufacturer of snowblowers and lawn mowers, used to follow standard "deny and defend" practices, and its product liability costs soared. But in 1991 it switched to a more conciliatory approach. Now, when the company hears about a product-related accident, it immediately sends staff members to visit the family. They begin by expressing regret: "Setting aside the question of who's at fault, we want you to know that we feel terrible that this happened. We're going to do our best to resolve this thing and make sure it doesn't happen again." Toro says the conciliatory approach has halved the time it takes to settle a claim and has cut the average cost from $115,000 in 1991 to $35,000 in 2004. Saying you're sorry when you make a mistake is not only the right thing to do, but it's often good business.

But a bad or late apology is worse than no apology at all. There is no substitute for the timely phrases, "I apologize" and "I'm sorry." Beyond that, an effective apology has four ingredients. Call it the Four Rs: Recognition, Responsibility, Remorse, and Restitution.

- *Recognition:* An apology needs to ensure that the injured party knows that the speaker understands specifically what he or she did wrong. "I recognize that over a dozen families were forced to evacuate their homes."
- *Responsibility:* An indication that the speaker accepts personal responsibility for the injury. "I accept responsibility for the error in judgment that forced over a dozen families to evacuate their homes."
- *Remorse:* A sincere "I apologize" or "I'm sorry." "I apologize to the people who were forced to leave their homes." It helps if the speaker can promise not to make the same mistake in the future.
- *Restitution:* Whenever practical, the apology should include an offer to make the injured parties whole. "We will reimburse the injured parties for all the costs associated with the forced evacuation of their homes, and the company will donate $100,000 to the town."

When I Had to Apologize

Like most of us, I'm sure I've uttered the words "I'm sorry" hundreds, maybe thousands, of times in my life. My parents, my children, my wife, and my friends all earned their share of apologies from me. But I was not conscious of the power of an apology in the corporate setting. I was afraid that an apology delivered in public acknowledged legal liability on behalf of the company I was a part of.

And then a manager at Lee Hecht Harrison made a huge ethical mistake. As it happened, the ethical lapse was quickly exposed. The *Wall Street Journal* wrote a long article about it. The paper had acquired an incriminating memo this manager wrote and published it on the front page for the world to see. People looked to me as one of the people who had his name on the door to see what I would do and say.

First a little background. By 1995, Lee Hecht Harrison had become a leader in the outplacement industry. As one of the top three outplacement companies in the United States, our reputation was and is one of integrity, professionalism, and ethical behavior. We had cofounded the industry's trade association in 1982 and had founded the professional association a few years later. One of the drivers of the latter development was the desire to collaborate with our industry colleagues in creating an official and specific set of ethics guidelines for the practice of outplacement. These guidelines included keeping confidences, avoiding conflicts of interest, setting realistic expectations, and placing paramount the interests of the job seekers who trust us to advise them.

In one instance we failed, and our failure became public. After much anguish I apologized. It wasn't easy, but it turned out to be the right thing to do.

Like most business disasters, this one was lubricated by the troublesome mix of external competition and internal pressure to win. Lee Hecht Harrison prevailed over two other competitors in the outplacement field to represent an international company. It was a coup for us, one of the larger contracts in our 20-year history. Our first assignment was to counsel about 175 sales and marketing people the employer separated when it combined two large divisions. Unfortunately, I soon learned that an overly aggressive Lee Hecht Harrison salesperson agreed to terms that were, from our perspective, clearly unethical. Nevertheless, our management controls failed, and we accepted the assignment. Tellingly, two competitors who were offered the same terms had declined the opportunity.

Just what was it we did that was so unethical? In our zealousness to serve the company which retained us (the sponsor company) and give Lee Hecht Harrison a competitive advantage, we violated a clear ethical boundary: to put the needs of the separated employee first. Instead, our actions appeared to put the needs of the sponsor company above those we were committed to serve. Specifically, the salesperson agreed to steer the outplaced employees away from competitors of the sponsor company. This misguided commitment played a prominent role in our being awarded the contract.

As the downsizing launch date grew closer, this salesperson issued a memo to the project delivery team which stated: "[The sponsor company] has expressed great concern about impacted employees accepting new positions with competitors. [The sponsor company] is relying on LHH to focus the employees on transferring his/her skills away from competitors and, if possible, outside the industry. While this will certainly be a challenge, LHH will be measured by the number of placements made away from competitors."

The article appeared on January 27, 1995. The headline read, "Memo Reveals Dual Allegiances of Outplacement Firm."

Our first instinct was to be defensive and minimize the event as an aberration. After cooler heads prevailed, we swung into crisis management mode. We eventually accepted the counsel of an experienced crisis management consultant who told us to step up to the challenge, accept full responsibility, and apologize. I credit him for stopping our defensiveness in its tracks and for encouraging us to focus on contrition. His advice: "Own up, face up, pay up—as if the entire firm were guilty!"

Our consultant was strong, uncompromising, and insistent that if we issued a broad-scale apology, our constituencies would understand. Moreover, it would start an active, ongoing, and healthy dialogue around personal and professional ethics in the outplacement industry. If we apologized, he told us, the brutal headlines would soon go away. We could get back to the business of what we do best: working on behalf of separated individuals who rely on us to act in their best interests. If we stonewalled, by contrast, the story would be kept alive, and the individuals whom we had failed would have to wait for the services we promised.

On February 1, 1995, I issued the following statement to all Lee Hecht Harrison clients, prospects, job seekers, and employees. We also published this statement.

Dear Friends and Colleagues:

On January 27, the *Wall Street Journal* published an article that criticized Lee Hecht Harrison for handling an outplacement assignment improperly.

The particular situation arose when we misinterpreted our sponsor company's concern about the non-compete agreements that many of their employees had signed. As the *Journal* pointed out, our offices were initially sent inappropriate guidance on this topic.

Despite our best efforts to verbally correct these instructions, it appears after further investigation that some people who came to us for help may have received guidance from us which was not in their best interests.

In light of concerns expressed by our employees, clients and sponsor companies who were surprised by the *Journal* article, we feel a need to state clearly the operating principles and values which have guided Lee Hecht Harrison for 20 years.

The Management of Lee Hecht Harrison deeply regrets that a lack of clear procedures may have fostered the impression that our firm is anything less than entirely ethical in its practice.

Therefore, today we are reiterating and setting forth the following policies to prevent such a failure from occurring in our organization in the future. And we will be visiting each of our offices in order to personally convey both the spirit and intent of this message:

1. Lee Hecht Harrison consultants are reminded that their first responsibility is to the people who are sent to us for help, to assist them in finding suitable new employment as quickly as possible.
2. Although consultants sometimes receive background information from sponsor companies and may provide feedback on the status of their former employees' job search efforts, such communication must in no way compromise the professionalism of the services we provide, or the employment options of the client.
3. All written communications to a sponsor company about an individual client's progress will be available to that client.
4. Lee Hecht Harrison General Managers are responsible for making certain the people we help are served according to both our firm's values as well as the Association of Outplacement Consulting Firms International's (AOCFI) Professional Code of Ethics.
5. As people begin service with Lee Hecht Harrison, they receive as part of their orientation materials a copy of the AOCFI's Professional Code of Ethics and a statement of our firm's operating principles so that they are aware of specific information on how to report immediately and

directly to Lee Hecht Harrison Senior Management should they have a grievance or a perception of unethical practices.

6. Lee Hecht Harrison General Managers will seek approval from their respective Regional Senior Vice Presidents before disseminating guidance to other offices which will impact our clients' job-finding options.

As a further step to assure the integrity of our practice, we will reach out to those individuals who received our services during this assignment to be certain that they feel satisfied and fairly treated. If, in fact, any job-seeker we were assisting believes that their Lee Hecht Harrison consultant acted as indicated in the 12/29/93 memo, or if any client received service from us as described in the *Journal* article, we would like to speak with him or her immediately to set the matter right.

We are seeking to learn important lessons from this experience. For example, we will review all our internal operating practices to ensure that they meet our rigorous standards. And we will continue to refine our procedures to assure that they measure up to our strong ethical and moral convictions.

Needless to say, when we deal with people whose lives, careers and families are as painfully affected as they are following separation of employment, we take our obligation to help them most seriously. Consequently, we are saddened and distressed that we may have fallen short of the high expectations of our employees, clients and sponsor companies. We are determined it will never happen again.

Sincerely,

Stephen G. Harrison
President

I was sure that this situation would be the death knell for our firm, a demoralizing episode from which our culture could never recover. But instead, almost without exception, we experienced a rush of congratulatory letters and faxes from customers, industry leaders, and journalists. Even the reporter who wrote the story and follow-up articles let me know that she admired our candor. And, far from going out of business, we had the best quarter in our history.

In retrospect, long before I had thought out the four critical elements of apology, my apology addressed each of the four elements. It recognized the *severity* of what we did, we took *responsibility* for the lapse, we expressed *remorse*, and we offered *restitution*. As for the reaction of our employees, I didn't wait for feedback. I personally visited each of our offices within a six-week period to say, "I'm sorry. Here's what we've learned. We'll be stronger as a result. We're bigger than any single mistake, and we will be a stronger company for it." Then I listened to employees as they talked about what the incident meant to them. The effect on me was painful and enduring.

LIVING IN TRUTH AND HUMILITY

There is a direct link between truth-telling and humility. It is not too big a leap for pompous executives to believe that their opinions are too important for the truth to matter. Pompous executives are vulnerable to shrinking from truths that threaten their privilege. In all such cases, not only do the individuals suffer, but so do their organizations. We are all entitled to our own opinions; we are not entitled to our own facts.

A leader's commitment to decency is tested every time he or she is faced with an inconvenient truth. Truth is the fundamental prerequisite for decency. In the absence of a collective commitment to honesty, well-intentioned and well-thought-out gestures will come to naught. "An ailing organization can open itself to new ideas, develop innovative and popular products, and share the fruits of its labors equitably among its members and constituents," say Robert Hardy and Randy Schwartz in *The Self-Defeating Organization*. "But if it continues to dissemble, speak in euphemisms, and withhold key information from concerned members, these efforts seldom make a lasting impact on an organization's long-term performance."

Charles (Chuck) Schwab, chairman of the brokerage firm that bears his name, has earned a reputation for telling the truth. "Clients will stick with you in good times and bad, as long as you tell them the truth," he not only said, but modeled over and over again.

A firm's commitment to truth-telling is often tested during adversity. Here's how Schwab handled a crisis when its very existence was at stake. On Friday, October 16, 1987, the stock market collapsed. It was the first day in which the Dow Jones

Industrial Average fell by more than 100 points in a single trading session. Schwab's computers were overwhelmed, and many customers could not execute sell orders, causing them to incur high losses. "There were times that day when stock traders felt as though they were standing outside their own bodies, watching themselves with a bizarre detachment as they frantically attempted to unload stocks," observes Joseph Nocera in his book *A Piece of the Action: How the Middle Class Joined the Money Class.* At Schwab, the computers were overwhelmed by 8 a.m. The Schwab toll-free phone system also fell victim to the incessant calls. For several days, the Schwab customers heard only busy signals.

Customers had a right to be upset, and they were. Chuck Schwab's response was notable. Instead of defending the company or making excuses, he apologized and quietly reimbursed thousands of customers for their losses. Schwab's propensity for admitting responsibility and making things right shone through. On October 28, 1987, investors opened the *Wall Street Journal* to see two full-page ads, one showed Chuck apologizing to customers for the mishaps and asking them for their patience. The other ad expressed appreciation to the thousands of Schwab employees who pulled together and took orders manually while technicians struggled to bring the computer system back up.

During the course of his or her career, every leader will be tested by adversity, and sometimes the leader will fail. At these times, employees and other stakeholders are watching very carefully. When they see the leader as a fallible person who makes mistakes and has the decency to acknowledge them, take responsibility, and apologize if appropriate, they will not abandon the leader. Followers demand neither flawlessness nor omniscience.

In fact, research shows that the most effective leaders selectively show their weaknesses. By exposing some vulnerability, they reveal their approachability and humanity. In the end, followers demand leaders who are worthy of being followed.

8

Separation Decencies

Every exit is an entry somewhere else.

TOM STOPPARD

In the 1970s, a new and unique service emerged—outplacement consulting. The service and its component firms were started by behavioral scientists, former clergy, and social service people as well as former HR people. The theory was to enable companies to facilitate change, especially people-change, by making it easier and more humane to separate people. Companies could contract with capable outside consultants who would take immediate responsibility for career-coaching the employee(s) affected by corporate downsizings.

During my first week at the firm that would become Lee Hecht Harrison, the original two partners invited me to a welcoming lunch. It was a time to talk philosophically about outplacement as a helping profession, not just as a business. Somewhere between the main course and the champagne good-luck toast, Bob Hecht said something that made a big impression on me. "The three greatest tragedies in a person's world are death, divorce, and job loss," he said. "And you'd be surprised how many people would place these in a very different priority order than I just did."

To many people, job loss is close to death because of how intimately we identify ourselves with what we do for a living. So we outplacement consultants find that at times it feels as if we save lives. At our best, we are *transfer of strength* agents. We transfer our strength to temporarily strength-depleted people; people who have lost not only their jobs, but also essential elements of their identity. The job seekers have lost both their salary income and their psychic income.

And with some, unfortunately, the loss of their job threatens their reason for being. Separated people can slip into depression, self-destructive behavior, and more rarely, into violence targeted at others. In many cultures, the risk of suicide associated with job loss is well known. In Japan, for example, it is estimated that there are as many as 100 suicides per day related to workplace stress and job loss. That risk of serious trauma following job loss is partly what gave birth to the outplacement industry.

DECENCY UNDER THE MICROSCOPE

Many companies do everything in their power to avoid layoffs. Sometimes economic realities make that approach impossible. When layoffs are imminent, small decencies can make all the difference. A simple managerial commitment to small decencies during and immediately following a layoff does nothing to interfere with the economic necessities that forced the layoff. Small decencies put into play during and after this most difficult of management tasks—the act of separating an employee—will signal a leader's sensitivity and caring, and a commitment to everyone who is watching. And here's a critical point. Everyone, and I mean everyone, is watching during and after a downsizing.

This is no time for managerial myopia. Employees may be separated, but it's not so easy to erase their memories. "Survivor's guilt" is a real and present issue that can be managed, but only if it is acknowledged. So, also, must retained employees face the soul-crushing, "Am I next?" fear that befalls retained employees after a downsizing. The culture's use of the word "survivor" to describe the state of people still employed after layoffs underscores the life-and-death stakes at work. Ignoring the fact that the retained employees have been affected can result in a long-lasting adverse impact on productivity and morale.

IT IS NEVER OVER

Leaders confront tremendous pressures during layoffs. One of the biggest temptations from every corner of the organization is to say, "It is over! There will be no more!" It's understandable to want to reassure. Leaders should resist this temptation. Leaders should tell the truth, even if the hard truth is the opposite of what some survivors want to hear. Retained employees desperately want to hear that the layoffs are over and that their jobs are safe.

"It is never over," says David Noer in *Healing the Wounds*. "This is as close to a law as anything I have found in the study of layoffs. The forces of the economy, the dynamics of technology, and the reality of the new employment contract make any kind of long-range employment promise an illusion."

DECENT GROUND RULES

I think one of the best ways to learn about separation decencies is to look at how other companies have approached layoffs.

Some stories give us role models; others give us warnings. In my opinion, one of the best-managed downsizings of the past few years was undertaken in 2001 by Agilent, an $8.3 billion spin-off of Hewlett-Packard. The company was faced with an economic downturn that hit the telecom industry especially hard. Agilent had inherited much of the full employment culture of Hewlett-Packard, an organization that had never had a layoff. This heritage made what Agilent had to do especially difficult. After postponing the inevitable by belt-tightening, slashing expenses, and even getting employees to accept a temporary 10 percent, across-the-board salary cut, Agilent was forced to eliminate 4,000 jobs—9 percent of the company.

If there were no alternatives to layoffs, so be it. But Ned Barnholt, now chairman emeritus, laid out three ground rules:

1. Employees were to be notified only by their direct managers.
2. Managers would be clear and honest.
3. Layoff decisions were to be based on published criteria.

Barnholt understood that the downsizing campaign had to be two parts communication to one part implementation. On August 20, 2001, the day Agilent would report a quarterly loss of $219 million—its first loss ever—Barnholt got on the public address system for the first time, according to a report in *Fortune*. Tradition was to be broken that day, and tradition was to be created. Barnholt insisted on making the announcement to employees himself so they wouldn't have to hear about it from the media. He presented the deteriorating state of the business, recognized the sacrifices employees had already made, and detailed how many people would lose their jobs, where the number came from, and how the admittedly painful process would work.

This direct personal announcement was a decency that started the process on the right foot. Going forward, Agilent made the process as transparent as possible, demonstrating another separation decency. The forms managers were to use in making selections were posted on Agilent's intranet. Employees could see the criteria on which the selection decisions would be made. Agilent considered the layoff regrettable, but nothing to be ashamed about. Rarely has such a large organization been as public with a layoff as was Agilent.

The second round of communications was to come from the managers actually making the difficult decisions. Barnholt sent more than 3,000 managers through a series of daylong training exercises, where they role-played and practiced the right and wrong ways to separate people. Managers were expected to be as honest as possible. The company wanted a maximum of fairness and a minimum of ambiguity in the process, and by all accounts, it succeeded. Many of the employees Agilent separated wrote Barnholt that they were satisfied with the fairness and decency, if not the outcome, of the process.

SEPARATION MAKES MEMORIES

Saying goodbye is sometimes a business reality. The decencies associated with the details of how we say goodbye become an important component of our corporate culture. When we separate people, we are constructing memory; memory for those separated and memory for our organizations.

A clear testimony to a culture of trust is how a company separates valued people. "We hate to see you go. Give us your cell phone and keys to the company car. Security will escort you out!" These sentences sometimes need to be said, but when uttered in juxtaposition, they send a message of hypocrisy not only to the separated employee but also to retained employees who will inevitably hear about it. I'm not ignoring that companies need to protect their assets. But it is simply neither decent nor prudent to use sloppy language at times of separation.

Certainly the company should protect itself by canceling passwords and retrieving keys, ID cards, cell phones, pagers, and so forth. But these steps need to be choreographed thoughtfully and in proportion to the situation. When an employee is fired for a cause such as embezzlement or harassment, it is entirely prudent for the company to block his or her access to networks and escort the employee off the premises. Any employee who has broken faith with the company cannot expect anything more. But if it's a no-fault separation (e.g., economic downturn or a consolidation) where there is no question about the employee's performance or integrity, then decency calls for a different set of actions. In these cases, anything that questions the employee's performance or integrity can and should be avoided.

In all cases, security personnel should remain in the background unless the employee has demonstrated a lack of integrity or propensity for violence. If you have regard for the employee you are about to separate, ask yourself this question: "Would I rehire this person if I could?" If the answer is yes, then I think the risk is worth taking. Let such people gather their personal possessions in dignity and in private. Is there a risk here? Sure. Behaving well is no guarantee that someone else will not behave badly. But it's the way to go.

PREPARATION, PREPARATION, PREPARATION

Separating an employee is too sensitive a situation to be handled without extensive advance planning. The entire episode, whether large or small scale, needs to be choreographed thoughtfully. It is not a time for a manager to be spontaneous. Managers do best when they receive separation training like that used at Agilent in the days immediately before the event. In these training sessions, managers learn what to say and what not to say. Managers are taught how to respond nonreactively and empathetically to an employee's emotional expressions, which can be intense. Managers are reminded how to listen, the decency we discuss in Chapter 6. In essence, the training helps the manager behave decently when the employee, understandably, may not.

No downsizing is perfect. There is often a slip, especially with large-scale workforce reductions, no matter how well you plan it. If there are 50 things that can go wrong in any downsizing and you think of 49 of them, you're a genius. But the one you miss can be devastating. That's why we are obliged to try to eliminate every opportunity for unnecessary offense. It's not easy. Here are just a few of the avoidable mistakes that I have seen.

In one case, we thought we had sufficiently trained and coached the terminating manager about how to break the news that an employee was losing his job. But when the time came, the terminating manager couldn't quite bring himself to utter the appropriate words clearly enough. He obviously failed to deliver the message because the individual who was to be separated returned to the job the following morning. There is a natural human tendency to avoid confrontation, so it's understandable that we pull back from using direct language. That's why training and coaching are imperative.

In another case, news of the impending layoff leaked out. This can be a real problem for an organization. If individuals learn of their upcoming separation through the newspaper, they are likely to have bitter feelings and may not even show up for their termination meetings. If local reporters get the story only from the voices of the separated employees, the company looks unprofessional and needs to do hurry-up damage control.

Another set of mistakes revolves around failing to be thoughtful about the day selected for the separation. All it takes is a phone call to avoid separating an employee:

- On his or her birthday or on the day before a milestone birthday (e.g., the day before the employee's fiftieth birthday)
- On a significant date such as the day before his or her pension plan vests
- On a religious holiday significant to minority employees
- When the separation documents are not in order
- When a company activity could interfere with the notification (e.g., "Bring Your Daughters to Work Day")

David Noer, author of *Healing the Wounds*, tells the story of a major company that embarked on a downsizing that resulted from a downturn in the company's fortunes. On the day of the downsizing, management neglected to check on something that unnecessarily rubbed salt into already open wounds. As the separated employees were leaving the building carrying boxes of their belongings, what they saw were gardeners actively at work redesigning the corporate landscape. The separated employees had just been told that economic belt-tightening required their separation. Imagine the resentment on the part of the departing employees as they saw hundreds of thousands of dollars being spent on the landscape. This situation could easily have been avoided.

There is no such thing as a good time to separate an employee. But some days and times are better than others. We don't recommend Fridays for a number of reasons. If corporate help such as outplacement is offered, it is not available on weekends. The employee separated on Friday has all weekend to stew without the opportunity to seek help. Experience shows that some employees separated on Fridays make tactical mistakes, such as panicking and firing off ill-considered e-mails or résumés. Sometimes family dynamics suffer when separated employees have too little support and too much time on their hands.

We don't recommend Mondays, either, and for a little-understood reason. Timing the notification on a Monday means that the managers have two days to forget the briefings they presumably received the prior week. Let's give a difficult process every chance to work.

All things considered, the optimum days for separating employees are Tuesdays, Wednesdays, and Thursdays.

Where the conversation takes place is also important. The supervisor's office may seem natural, but it presents a number of problems. First, if the employee becomes upset or needs some time for composure, there is no place for the employee to go. For the manager to leave his or her own office so the separated employee can regain his or her composure is not practical.

The alternative of forcing a shaken and embarrassed employee to walk the gauntlet past coworkers is risky on a number of levels. If the separated employee's coworkers do not know what happened, they may make an embarrassing mistake, such as engaging the person in a work conversation. If they do know, the passing of the separated employee will be as uncomfortable for them as for the individual. In general, it's best to give the news in the separated employee's office or a vacant office. These locations also make it convenient for outplacement consultants or other supportive individuals to join the employee immediately after the notification.

Firing an employee in the employee parking lot will make for a long-lasting bitter taste. Similarly, severing an employment relationship at a bar or restaurant will have a counterproductive effect. Both are too public, and neither provides the environment for the notifying manager to behave with decency and sensitivity.

Thoughtful companies also consider the employee's logistical issues like transportation. Many companies encourage car-pooling. But if the employee to be separated is a member of a car pool, there are two issues that must be considered. First, will the employee want to ride with others on this difficult day? Second, if the employee is expecting to ride with the car pool at the end of the day, there's a big issue if the separation occurs early in the day. The employee may be stuck. Likewise, if the separation notification happens minutes before the on-site child-care center closes, the separated employee may be rushed to pick up a child. The most decent approach is to assign someone—a person from HR or an outplacement consultant, perhaps—to help the employee resolve logistical issues for that day. This person should check in with the employee as soon as he or she has gained composure in order to eliminate as much logistical stress as possible.

I encourage you not to underestimate the amount of choreography that has to go into a well-planned, sensitive, and decent separation notification. Decency begins with training the managers. It involves picking the right time and place for the notifications and having the right support systems in place immediately after the notifications. Decency also calls for support of the notification managers throughout their difficult day. While some companies have the staff and skills to attend to all these details themselves, an increasing number of companies turn to career management companies to handle the planning and immediate ramifications of notifications. They can never be the key players: company managers have to notify the employees personally. But they can be choreographers to help them put the pieces together with effectiveness and decency.

THE BEST-LAID PLANS

Maybe one way to emphasize the need for planning is to show what can happen when important decency details are not considered in advance. RadioShack Corp. earned itself a world of bad publicity by sending an e-mail notifying about 400 workers that they were being dismissed. The separated employees at the Fort Worth, Texas, headquarters all received the same e-mail on a Tuesday morning. The messages read: "The workforce reduction notification is currently in progress. Unfortunately your position is one that has been eliminated."

Bloggers quickly picked up the story. Within days, customers around the world erupted in fury, vowing that they would never shop at RadioShack again. Company officials defended themselves by saying that employees had been told in a series of meetings that layoff notices would be delivered electronically. The electronic notification was quicker and allowed more privacy than breaking the news in person, according to company spokesperson Kay Jackson.

People were offended by RadioShack's impersonal approach, and what they perceived, right or wrong, as the disingenuous way it defended its method as being in the interests of those dismissed. Laying people off is not easy. Most managers say telling people they are being separated is the most difficult part of their jobs. So it's understandable that managers want to protect themselves from this painful chore. But it's precisely because the chore is so painful—and all the pain is borne by the soon-to-be-former colleague—that decency is required.

By the way, RadioShack also gave notice to president and chief executive David Edmondson at about the same time as these layoffs. Edmondson was forced to admit to "misstatements" on his résumé following a story in the *Fort Worth Star-Telegram* questioning whether his résumé was accurate in listing two degrees from Pacific Coast Baptist Bible College. In the wake of a series of high-profile corporate scandals, the quick acceptance of his resignation spotlights how ethical considerations have become increasingly important in today's business environment.

THE DECENT NOTIFICATION

The conversation between a manager and person being separated is the most critical piece of the separation puzzle. I want to emphasize two core management decencies associated with this conversation:

1. Take time with the employee. A short, rushed, or interrupted meeting is salt in the wound.
2. Listen to the employees with empathy and without reacting. If you're anxious or defensive, it may be even harder to be silent

while the employee talks. But, as we've seen, you can't listen and talk at the same time. If the employee is critical of the company or even of your management, you shouldn't debate the issue. Remember, listening is not the same as agreeing.

Separating an employee is not a time for a protracted performance review. Nor is it a time for reflective philosophical conversations and platitudes such as, "I know how you must feel" or "This is as difficult for me as it is for you." Rather, a brief conversation, to the point, delivered courteously and succinctly, will communicate the reality of a decision that has been made and is irrevocable. If confirmation of the employee's severance entitlements is delivered in writing at the same time, it avoids much potential for misunderstanding.

SEPARATION LANGUAGE

What word do you apply to individuals who are let go? The choice of words signals attitudes. An organization that talks about "term-inees" or "rightsized employees" is likely to have a much different culture from one that uses words such as "former colleague" or "separated employee." When someone at W.L. Gore quits or is let go, the company refers to it as a separation. "This word acknowledges that a mind and a heart are leaving the organization, and it speaks to the relationship side of the separation instead of only to the procedure," write Scott Cawood and Rita Bailey in *Destination Profit*. The separation of an employee can best be explained as part of an organization's reputation bank account. Sometimes there are deposits, and sometimes there are withdrawals. Each separation should be treated directly, with candor and honesty.

In any case, the objective should be less about finding the perfect euphemism and more about avoiding expressions that stray from the truth. Euphemisms are likely to backfire. Here are a few most of us are familiar with: downsized, reengineered, and rightsized.

Let me say a word about the reference statement. This is the language that the ex-employer will release to parties considering hiring the separated employee. It is almost always in everyone's interest to negotiate the content of this statement. No matter what the circumstances of an employee's departure, the former company would like to see the separated employee reemployed as quickly as possible. The former employee, of course, would like to be employed as quickly as possible. The reference statement should not be an obstacle to this shared interest. The content of the separation statement should be negotiated as generously as the facts permit. That's where decency comes in. Human resources and former managers must be trained to release the separation statement without further comment or embellishment.

TELL THE TRUTH

Telling the truth requires two separate commitments. First is the commitment to accept the truth for oneself. Second is the commitment to tell the truth to others. For me, the first commitment is often the hardest.

Whether speaking with those being separated or those being retained, it's important that managers tell the truth, even when it's not what either of these groups wants to hear. While it might be tempting to tell a separated employee that there may be another job for him or her in a few months, that's rarely the truth and will only heighten expectations and discourage people from finding new work quickly. Retained employees want a commitment that they will not be next, but it is dangerous to make such promises. No matter how much it seems to hurt in the short term, in the long run it is always less painful to have had the truth up front.

Using facts is a great way to deliver the truth. They may not always be convenient. Sometimes the facts are unpalatable. And during layoffs, facts can be downright ugly. Nevertheless, both separated and retained employees are always better off in authentic relationships that by their very nature boldly embrace the facts. Everyone, whether separated or still employed, needs to take individual responsibility for his or her job security and career destiny. It's impossible to do that without candid, fact-based conversations.

To summarize, the minimum requirements for decency in employee separation include the following five values:

1. A fair and preferably transparent selection process. This means objective, easily understood standards.
2. A sensitive, in-person notification meeting with the immediate supervisor of the separated individual.
3. Sensitivity to the logistics of the notification process.
4. Sensitivity around the reference statement. The separated individual should know exactly what the company will tell potential employers. This should be in writing so both parties are satisfied.
5. Management accessibility to retained employees.

DIGNITY AND DECENCY

People have come to terms with job loss as a fact of commercial life. What people have not come to terms with, and will never forgive, is when the orchestration of the downsizing event comes off as anything but well-thought-out, with a focus on individual dignity.

We are obliged to try to minimize the risk of anything giving inadvertent offense to individual dignity. Employees always sense decency and its converse. In an environment of decency, separated employees will tend to accept the decision and move on much more easily. When unnecessary indignities color the separation event, separated employees will remember the indignity long after they have come to accept the separation.

Part Three

Building the Decent Organization

A master potter had a dream of a bold new glaze for his delicate porcelain vases. It became the central focus of his work and life. Every day he experimented with new formulas and compounds, feverishly attempting to duplicate on his pots the glaze he envisioned. His efforts went on for years, but the potter could not find the proper combination of chemistry and temperature to achieve the finish he sought. Eventually, after decades of work, the exhausted master potter decided that he had nothing left to try. So he tended the flames of his kiln to a white heat and walked into the inferno. When the kiln finally cooled and the master's horrified assistants opened up the gate, all they found was the master's last batch of vases. And the perfection of the glaze! It was precisely the exquisite finish the master potter had long been striving for. Its creation required the master himself to disappear into his creations.

I've noticed that when members of a team that produces truly spectacular results (think the Apple Macintosh or iPod) talk about the experience, the terms they often use is how wonderful it feels to be consumed by the project. The master potter expressed this literally. I'm not in favor of employees immolating themselves. But on a metaphorical level, I believe most of us long to have such meaning in our work that we would sacrifice for it. Like the master potter, members of teams that produce outstanding results offer themselves in the service of the work.

When we are passionate about our work, we become part of the work and the work becomes part of us. To many employees, the highest expression of their commitment is to make a difference by doing good work. They create meaning by making a difference. Decencies fuel the transformation of ordinary, everyday forms into the exquisite and the rare. They are the way for individuals and organizations to express and even sustain the meaning that sustains them.

9
Bigger
Decencies

The ideal in life is only in small part due to bold public action by important people. All the rest of this force is made of small and obscure deeds. But the sum of these is a thousand times stronger than wide large acts of those who receive wide public recognition.

ALBERT SCHWEITZER

If a business process or gesture proves to be novel, interesting, and effective, the tendency in most organizations is to repeat it. So it is with small decencies. As soon as a small decency is recognized for the gem that it is, the next step is to try it again under the same circumstances and then under slightly different circumstances, and if it still continues to work, under varied circumstances. From there it is a short leap to give it a name, appoint a manager, write a policy, and assign a budget. All of a sudden, a small decency that was free and spontaneous becomes a program. The gesture ceases to be an expression of an individual's values and aims to be an expression of organizational values. It slips out of one person's control and into the system. The gesture can become separated from its intrinsic meaning and, ultimately, devoid of meaning. It can become habit instead of passion.

My point is not that institutionalizing small decencies is undesirable. As small decencies morph into bigger decencies, something certainly is lost, but something certainly is gained as well. At its best, institutionalization keeps the ripples of decencies expanding outward from the source, creating bigger impacts throughout the enterprise and beyond. It is precisely this process that allows small decencies to change corporate culture.

INSTITUTIONALIZING THE SMALL DECENCY

All decencies exist on a continuum of size from small to bigger. As decencies become bigger, as they become something that companies, not simply individuals, do, they tend to become perceived as more newsworthy. For that reason, it's pretty easy to look on company Web sites, in printed reports, or in the media to find examples of big decencies the companies or their observers find valuable. What I find most interesting are ideas that probably started as small decencies, but in their present manifestation have evolved into something bigger. I also appreciate company programs that encourage individuals to act with decency. The examples below are only a small sampling of big decencies I've run across in the workplace. Companies undertake big decencies outside their company walls, too. Some people have a name for these big decencies: corporate social responsibility (CSR). I say more about CSR and its relation to small decencies later in this chapter. Meanwhile, let's take a look at some gestures that probably started out as small decencies and have since become big decencies.

Rules Are Meant to Be Decent—
Southwest Airlines and Ritz-Carlton

Decencies sometimes require breaking rules. Work rules are important, but strict adherence to rules often becomes an excuse for laziness or complacency. "A foolish consistency is the hobgoblin of little minds," Emerson said, with an emphasis more on *foolish* than *consistency*. At Southwest Airlines, all rules (except safety rules) are up for grabs if an employee can justify why they shouldn't be applied. When applicants for customer-facing jobs are interviewed, they are asked, "Tell us about a time when you broke a rule to help a customer." If applicants can't offer a specific example of how they willfully broke a rule to help a customer, they are not hired.

Trusting employees with more discretion about when to enforce rules and when to relax creates a good experience for everyone. Every employee of a Ritz-Carlton hotel, from the concierge who speaks four languages to the housekeeper who cleans your room, has the authority, without manager involvement, to spend up to $2,000 to solve a guest's problem. Think about it: any Ritz-Carlton employee can spend more money than some earn in a month to solve a customer problem. Do you trust your employees with that much empowerment?

Of course, the Ritz-Carlton hotels invest substantially in their employees. All recruits go through tests that screen them for the attributes of the most successful Ritz employees. Ritz has learned that applicants whose test scores resemble those of its most exemplary employees tend to succeed. After employees are hired, training and coaching are constant. The result is not surprising. The Ritz-Carlton brand stands for perhaps the best hotel experience in the world. Ritz-Carlton hotels are so legendary for their reliable level of customer service that the chain received the coveted Malcolm Baldrige National Quality Award. As customers we may see a small decency when the bellhop gives us a bottle of water so that we can have something to drink during our taxi ride; the gesture is, in reality, an expression of a big, programmatic decency.

Reduce Mileage, Keep the Savings—Daniels Company

In an effort to reduce both turnover and expenses, the Daniels Company, a trucking firm in Springfield, Missouri, challenged its drivers to cut their fuel costs by improving mileage. Drivers got to keep the difference. Since then, employee turnover has been reduced by 25 percent and trucks are logging fewer miles, thus cutting overall costs. This big decency helps fight global warming too.

Rolling in the Dough—General Mills

Teams within the food products manufacturer General Mills celebrate when safety records are achieved. A lighthearted approach was used when the 500 workers at the Joplin, Missouri, plant, which produces frozen dough, achieved a first-in-history milestone for the corporation: seven million hours worked without a lost-time accident! Known as "Team Joplin," the employees had not sustained an accident that caused missed work since December 30, 1996. Anticipating the record, more than 100 of the male workers started growing beards prior to the seven-million-hour achievement.

Upon achieving the milestone, many employees, including the plant manager, clipped the number seven in their beards. Other employees proudly displayed Big G and Doughboy temporary tattoos. Local coverage of the event was made available through Champions TV. For the milestone, Team Joplin employees won the Champions Awards, which were personally presented to them by the CEO. Throughout the year, other facilities commemorated no-lost-time accident records as well with varied celebrations, from meals served up by the leadership team for all shifts to complimentary dinner theaters enjoyed with a guest to a day off for all employees on the date of the achievement. General Mills has one of the lowest employee injury rates among food industry companies.

Job Mentoring/Shadowing—Metso Minerals

When a new employee joins your company, assign an established employee to mentor him or her. Many companies have mentoring programs, and I think there is no better way to make new employees feel welcomed, comfortable, and effective from day one. Optimum results come when the mentors are volunteers, according to Dawna Smeltzer, manager of aftermarket services at Metso Minerals Industries. At her company, new employees shadow the mentor for six months after they are hired. The aim of the program is to facilitate skills transfer and to get the new employee integrated within the department and the company as effectively as possible. The company benefits in two broad ways. "First, new employees become productive much more quickly," Smeltzer says. The mentoring also contributes to a high retention level. Employees who are frustrated or are having difficulties can often go to their mentor. Metso's turnover rate is much lower than the industry average. Second, the company benefits because the job shadowing is good for the mentor too. "It's a huge investment, but it signals our commitment to their success," Smeltzer adds. "We have found that the best way to solidify a set of skills is by teaching them to somebody else."

Bright Ideas—Baptist Health Care

The Great Place to Work Institute has a repository of workplace decency stories. One program it has highlighted is the Bright Ideas program at Baptist Health Care, which solicits innovative ideas from all people throughout the organization, giving employees an opportunity to share thoughts, suggestions for improvement, and cost-savings ideas. Any idea that helps a department operate more efficiently or makes life easier for the customer is a Bright Idea. Employees submit their ideas directly into the Bright Ideas database. Their leader is responsible for implementing the idea, forwarding the idea to the most appropriate leader for implementation, or providing feedback to the originator on why the idea won't or can't be implemented.

Besides being the repository of initial submissions, the database also serves as a warehouse of ideas that all leaders can access to see if a solution to a problem they are experiencing was solved in another area. Leaders can also simply review ideas in the database to identify great suggestions for ways of doing things better.

Employees are recognized for submitting their ideas with "Food for Thought" (free meal) certificates, and they receive 10 points for ideas that are implemented. The points are redeemable for prizes, from a small lightbulb pin (10 points) to a director's chair (150 points). All employees are encouraged to propose at least two Bright Ideas each year.

Hal Hotline—Rosenbluth Travel

Rosenbluth Travel, the Philadelphia-based travel service company, prides itself on an open decision-making culture. One aspect of this is a structure that encourages all employees ("associates" in Rosenbluth parlance) to offer their ideas on how to improve the company, from how to do things in their own areas to worldwide policies and strategies.

The "Hal Hotline" is a voice-mail link that any associate can access to leave a message directly for Hal Rosenbluth. Rosenbluth promises to respond personally to every message. On one level, Hal's Hotline is really an electronic suggestion box. But it has two advantages over the old approach. It is much more active and relationship-driven. It's not just about an employee offering a suggestion to some anonymous committee. This offers employees a direct channel to the chairman. It also serves as a means for Rosenbluth to keep his fingers on the pulse of the company in an important way.

The Spirit of Fred Award—Disney

At Walt Disney World in Orlando, Florida, one of its 180 recognition programs is called "The Spirit of Fred Award," named for an employee named Fred. When Fred first went from an hourly to a salaried position, five people taught him the values necessary for success at Disney. This experience helped to inspire the award, and the name "Fred" became an acronym for Friendly, Resourceful, Enthusiastic, and Dependable. First given as a lark, the award has come to be highly coveted in the organization. Fred makes each award—a certificate mounted on a plaque, which he then varnishes—as well as the Lifetime Fred Award—a bronze statuette of Mickey Mouse given to those who have won several Spirit of Fred Awards. Here, one employee's decency is elevated to a structured program that still retains a personal touch.

World of Thanks—AT&T Universal Card Services

AT&T Universal Card Services in Jacksonville, Florida, uses the World of Thanks Award as one of more than 40 recognition and reward programs. It's a pad of colored paper shaped like a globe with "thank you" written all over it in different languages. Anyone in the company can write a message of thanks to someone else and send it to that person. The program is extremely popular: in four years the company has sent over 130,000 such notes. That's 130,000 small decencies rolled into one big decency program.

The Wingspread Award—Office of Personnel Management

The Office of Personnel Management in Washington, DC, uses an award that was first given to the division's special performer. Later that person passed the award to another person who, he believed, truly deserved it. The award came to take on great value and prestige because it came from one's peers. A recipient can keep the award as long as he or she wants, or until he or she discovers another special performer. When the award is to be passed on, a ceremony and lunch are planned.

The Golden Banana Award—Hewlett-Packard

A Hewlett-Packard company engineer burst into his manager's office in Palo Alto, California, to announce he'd just found the solution to a problem the group had been struggling with for many weeks. His manager quickly groped around his desk for some item to acknowledge the accomplishment and ended up handing the employee a banana from his lunch with the words, "Well done. Congratulations!" (How's that for a spontaneous, no-cost gesture of appreciation? A smaller decency there never was.) The first employee so honored was understandably puzzled, but eventually the charm of the gesture proved irresistible, and the next time someone did something noteworthy, people looked around for a banana. Over time the institutionalized Golden Banana Award became one of the most prestigious honors bestowed on an inventive employee.

Employees on Annual Report Cover—Nucor

One of the ways Nucor Corporation demonstrates its culture of egalitarianism is its practice of listing every Nucor employee, in alphabetical order, on the cover of its annual report. Now, if employees saw this practice as a gimmick of a company that otherwise does nothing to respect employees, then it would certainly backfire. The practice of listing names on the annual report must be in harmony with other practices that reinforce the organization's core values. At Nucor, the practice is not only unsurprising but an organic outgrowth of its employee-centered culture.

Surprise Breaks—Crate and Barrel

Crate and Barrel store managers in Houston began a program for their associates involving a "surprise hour off." Once a week, each store manager picks a sales associate and takes his or her shift on the floor for an hour saying, "You've been working hard, and I appreciate it. Enjoy a paid hour off. Come back refreshed and ready to sell more." The program gives the manager permission to offer what the manager probably sees as a nice gesture. The sales associate sees it as a small decency.

Early Friday Closing—Holder Construction Company

Holder Construction Company, a medium-sized company in Atlanta, Georgia, closes at 3:30 p.m. every Friday to allow associates to get an early start on the weekend. On the day before a holiday such as Memorial Day or Thanksgiving, offices close at 2 p.m., in recognition that many associates will be traveling and in order to allow them more time with family and friends. For a gesture that probably sacrifices much less productive time than the actual hours involved, it has an impact that carries over into the holidays as people talk about it. It's a decency that keeps on giving.

Work Shift Decency—East Alabama Medical Center

East Alabama Medical Center empowers employees at every level. For example, it lets employees and work groups choose their own shifts. A hospital has to run 24 hours, 7 days a week, including holidays, and that obligation creates an enormous scheduling burden for management. Some shifts are always more desirable than others. The Medical Center solves this problem in a unique way: supervisors don't impose a schedule. Instead, workers come together, figure out what shifts have to be covered, and self-select to fill them out of a sense of community. By transferring responsibility for this difficult management process to the workers who are most affected by it, management allows workers to take ownership of the task.

Quiet Room—Levi Strauss

Levi Strauss & Company has a quiet room where an employee can take a solitary break to relax, rest, meditate, or read. It is decent in both its simplicity and in its empathy.

CORPORATE SOCIAL RESPONSIBILITY: DECENCY OR DECEPTION?

Where is the line between workplace decency and the provision of basic human rights for workers? The preservation of human rights for workers is a cornerstone of many published CSR programs. By CSR, I mean a company's obligation to be sensitive to the needs of all the stakeholders. A company's stakeholders are all those who are influenced by, or who can influence, a company's decisions and actions. These typically include shareholders, employees, customers, joint venture partners, suppliers and vendors, the communities in which the company operates, and, increasingly, the general environment we all share. CSR is linked with the principles of "sustainable development" in proposing that economic enterprises have a duty to do more than maximize profits: they should also consider the social and environmental impacts of their operations.

While decencies big and small obviously go hand in hand with any organization committed to CSR, I believe that decencies work on a different level from that of CSR programs. The best CSR programs, like the best decencies, grow out of a company's values. But more fundamentally, decencies stem from an individual's values. While small decencies sometimes develop into big decencies, and while some leaders have the budgetary discretion and authority to make gestures that end up being big, decencies are at heart about an individual's commitment to do the right thing. Because of this grounding, I cannot conceive an effective, authentic CSR program in the absence of a culture of small decencies.

This insight came to me one morning in the spring of 2005. I had stopped at a Starbucks on the way to work. Sitting on the table with the milk and sugar were four separate sets of Starbucks brochures. One was a general promotional brochure and another solicited customer feedback. But the other two had little to do with Starbucks' products. One was called "Starbucks—In Our Communities," and the other, "Starbucks' Commitment to Social Responsibility . . . Beyond the Cup."

Instead of promoting "Frappuccinos," Starbucks used this valuable counter real estate to address employee volunteerism, charities, grants to organizations that are aligned with its literacy mission commitment (like "Jump Start," to reach preschool children in low-income communities), conservation, partnership with CARE (the relief organization), toy campaigns for children suffering from serious illness, and various food donations of unsold pastries.

The CSR brochure emphasized the company's commitment to ethics, financing for struggling coffee farmers, disaster relief, renewable energy, recycling, benefits for new adoptive parents, and employee and supplier diversity. Starbucks has received its share of criticism for the impact of its operations on both the growers that harvest the coffee it buys and the neighborhood coffee shops it is accused of driving out of business. Perhaps the company's CSR programs are a defensive effort to blunt its critics. Or maybe it's an altruistic response to the issues of globalization, economic inequality, and poverty. I don't know, and I really don't care. A company's motives are irrelevant if the CSR programs it undertakes truly help heal the world.

Clearly, Starbucks considers CSR to be part of its brand. But the main delivery mechanism for its brand is the thousands of baristas who take orders and deliver complicated coffees all day long. If my experience with the employees had been anything but decent—if the people behind the counter had not treated me with respect and kindness—then the CSR material would have been disingenuous. Likewise, if the management does not treat employees with decency, the monetary commitment to CSR would be meaningless.

By this measure, Starbucks is doing well. Starbucks employees are generally highly trained, empowered, and treated well. All employees (even part-time employees) get health-care coverage and profit sharing, benefits almost unheard of in similar retail businesses employing mostly entry-level workers. In response, Starbucks baristas are known for going the extra mile for customers.

I previously mentioned John Sifonis, the former Cisco executive, who brought coffee to his administrative assistant as a decency. Sifonis is addicted to Starbucks coffee. Wherever he is in the world, he is in a Starbucks store at least three times a day. He likes the coffee just fine—his drink of choice is a four-shot espresso—but what Sifonis really likes is the personal, professional, and friendly service. He especially likes the ability of the staff to recognize customers and remember their names. On one particular morning, before Sifonis could order his drink, his cell phone rang and he stepped out of line and went outside the store to deal with the call. When the barista saw that the call Sifonis was on was going to last a while, she came outside and presented Sifonis with a four-shot espresso. "That was a fantastic decency," Sifonis gushed. "She recognized me, understood my situation, remembered my preference, went out of her way to bring me what I wanted, and never worried about getting paid at the moment. This is more than delivering a great customer experience. It's a decency."

My point is that Starbucks' commitment to employee empowerment through benefits and training is part and parcel of its CSR initiatives. These programs, in turn, help create a culture that empowers baristas to deliver a great experience for customers like Sifonis. The Starbucks experience of CSR on a global scale and small decencies for an individual customer converge to make the brand as powerful and successful as it is.

Not everyone is convinced that CSR adds value to corporations. Some businesspeople still hold with Calvin Coolidge that the business of business is business. By this view, advocated by such worthies as Milton Friedman, who was awarded the Nobel Prize for Economics, a business serves society best by delivering the best possible returns on the investments entrusted to it. Out of those returns, individual investors are in the best position to support the causes and philanthropies that in their estimation are most deserving. By this logic, CSR programs that do not deliver obvious results to the bottom line are akin to giving away shareholders' money.

People who still hold this view are increasingly in the minority. There has been a CSR revolution in the last 15 years, says David Vogel, a professor at the University of California, who has studied the subject for 30 years. According to Vogel, corporations defend the value of CSR in many dimensions: CSR is in their business interests, they want to avoid difficulties with regulators, the practice resonates with employees and capital markets, it promotes sound talent management. Carried to an extreme, CSR is viewed by its advocates as "the survival of the virtuous."

But, he notes, there is no conclusive business case for CSR. Even consumers who could be impressed by the inclusion of a CSR component in a company's brand proposition tend to be motivated in their buying decisions by other considerations, such as price and availability. The financial markets are indifferent as well. Vogel is struck by the fact that during the year he was writing his book *The Market for Virtue*, not a single issue of *Business Investor's Daily* had any reference to CSR at all.

Vogel suggests that, "There is no evidence that firms without strong reputations for social responsibility find it more difficult or must pay higher salaries to attract first-rate, highly committed employees. Nor is there any evidence that the morale or commitment of these employees is less than in firms with better CSR reputations."

Yet, Vogel notes that Starbucks, in offering health care for all part-time as well as full-time employees, spends more on health-care coverage than on coffee beans. Does it need to do this? Would a cup of coffee cost the consumer less if Starbucks concerned itself with coffee only? In Starbucks' case, the practice of engaging the broad needs of its associates was established because its founder, Howard Schultz, was convinced that it is the decent thing to do. That's all the business case he needs. More than any leaflet, this policy and Schultz's lucidity about it tells me that Starbucks' CSR programs grow more from a culture of decencies than a defensive posture.

In Chapter 11, we'll see how several leaders are decency champions. One of these is Reuben Mark, chairman and CEO of Colgate-Palmolive. He made a decision to engage Colgate employees in the resurrection of a failing school. This was an act of decency—not grandiose CSR. Herb Kelleher's decision to fly senior citizens to their families during the holiday season is an act of decency, not philanthropy.

These acts and others like them are gestures that have an impact on the corporate culture within the company involved. The impact comes from crystal clear role modeling on the part of the leader and from the profound message sent by significant monetary investment. Not insignificantly, people believe what others say about them; if programs garner positive press, employees want to fill the shoes made of good impressions. All in all, these programs help employees understand the company's values. Above all, they understand something more about the organizational culture: what is expected and what is possible. When employees act in ways consistent with this understanding, an ethical culture is at least reinforced, if not created. If hypocrisy doesn't interrupt this process, the big programs—call them big decencies or CSR—have had the desired effect of molding a culture that is more inclined to comply with both legislation and public expectations alike.

I am convinced that we do the best not only for our companies, but also for our society, when we express what's important to us through genuine actions, be they small gestures or large acts of courage and principle. "Corporations not only have citizens, they are citizens," says Charles Handy, author of *The Hungry Spirit*. "We increasingly expect our corporate citizens to act decently. Some would argue that behaving decently is justifiable because it is, in the long run, good for the bottom line. A company that is mean and spiteful, and ungenerous to its surrounding communities, will only have fair-weather friends. Therefore, an investment beyond the call of duty which builds friends for hard times is a good investment."

CSR is not about altruism. The corporate citizen can be a force for positive change in the world, and not because positive change is good for the world but because positive change is good for the business. Charles Handy tells the story of a refinery in Australia which was beset by such a high level of absenteeism among its workers that productivity suffered. At the same time, the company was approached to contribute to a fund for the improvement of the local community. The managers of the refinery agreed, but added the following condition: for every day that absenteeism exceeded a certain level, the company would subtract a certain percentage of its donation. This condition was announced to all workers. "Within months the absenteeism had fallen to record low levels," Handy reported. "Individuals care, it seems, and companies should care also, if they are to represent the concerns of their members."

We lead responsibly by recognizing, each of us, his or her own obligation to set a proper example. We change our companies and, at our best, the world simply by acts of decency repeated as often as necessary.

Decency in Developing CSR Programs

Because the best CSR programs are those that channel not only organizational but also individual values, leaders will want to involve as many people as reasonable in deciding which activities should be undertaken or funded. Here are two ways I've seen of doing just that:

1. Involve employees at every level, include them in the decision about which initiatives to support. It's helpful for employees to have a voice in this decision because they will then be more engaged in making the investment a success. When a company selects causes and organizations to support, it can be helpful to survey the employees. Here's an example of constructive collaboration. When the Adecco Group was formulating its code of conduct, it wanted to append an Adecco values statement. A committee proposed 11 values and sent out the selections to 25,000 employees. Based on feedback from that mailing, the company selected a values statement that resonated with the most respondents.

2. Decentralize some of the company's CSR initiatives. This way, employees get to be directly involved in issues that have a local impact. International projects and significant philanthropies that are best managed at the corporate level can be important, but investing in local initiatives will fuel deep pride among employees and have great impact within the areas where you do business.

10

Toward Great Places to Work

When your work speaks for itself, don't interrupt.

HENRY J. KAISER

To my mind, no organization focuses more on the role of corporate culture as an enabler of business success than the Great Place to Work Institute, the firm that generates the data and selects companies for *Fortune* magazine's celebrated "100 Best Companies to Work For" issue. The San Francisco–based organization has been led since 1997 by cofounders Amy Lyman and Robert Levering.

I'm devoting a chapter to the work of the Great Place to Work Institute because it has so conspicuously made business decencies one of its selection standards. The institute is a globally respected organization that loudly celebrates corporate thoughtfulness, cultural sensitivity, and business decencies as critical components of business success. A measure of the organization's credibility is evidenced by the number of companies that accept its philosophy and selection criteria. These corporations commit considerable time, money, and other resources to be recognized by the Great Place to Work Institute because they perceive value in aligning themselves with its standards and the recognition that comes from being listed.

And what exactly does a company need to do to be considered for a spot on the Best Companies list? Once a company's nomination has been accepted, there are two data collection activities that occur. The first involves a confidential survey of a group of 400 randomly selected employees from the applying company. Known as the Trust Index, the survey was developed based on original research conducted for the two editions of the *100 Best Companies to Work For in America* books. Results of this survey are actually the most significant information used to determine if a company is among the 100 best. The perceptions of employees, as measured by the survey and captured in their comments, contribute approximately two-thirds of a company's overall score.

The second data collection activity involves the completion of a Culture Audit, which collates statistical information about policies and practices and asks for essays in response to a series of questions about company practices and the philosophy behind them. The Culture Audit reflects corporate data and a management point of view. It provides evidence from the leaders of the organization about their commitments to employees, shareholders, and the wider community. It also provides a comparative point of view for the employee survey data. A company can present a very strong Culture Audit, listing numerous employee benefit programs and progressive policies and practices, but it can also receive low levels of positive response from employees on the Trust Index. That contradiction is a big red flag in the application, because it signals a disconnect between policies and the actual experiences of work.

But for the companies that make it onto the list—the best companies, if you will—the trust promise is fulfilled. Sometimes it is fulfilled in grand style, but more often it is through the practice of simple actions that reinforce the organization's culture and meet employees' expectations about how they will be treated. The institute evaluates how the promise is fulfilled and combines this analysis with the employee survey to generate a score for each company. The 100 companies with the highest scores are featured in *Fortune* magazine.

The companies on the top list of best places to work enjoy a lot of bragging rights. But they enjoy much more. Increasingly, the practices that earn these companies a place on the list help them attract the best talent and retain that talent. For these companies, earning a spot on the list is considered an investment, not a cost. Here are the top 10 best companies to work for the last two years. Note that while there is considerable overlap from year to year, a company that has not been in the top 10 can suddenly find itself number one.

10 Best Companies to Work For

2006	2007
1. Genentech	Google
2. Wegmans Food Markets	Genentech
3. Valero Energy	Wegmans Food Markets
4. Griffin Hospital	Container Store
5. W.L. Gore & Associates	Whole Foods Market
6. Container Store	Network Appliance
7. Vision Service Plan	S.C. Johnson & Son
8. J.M. Smucker Company	Boston Consulting Group
9. Recreational Equipment (REI)	Methodist Hospital System
10. S.C. Johnson & Son	W.L. Gore & Associates

For me, though, the end goal isn't necessarily to make it onto this list or to achieve a high score on the institute's rigorous test. The end goal for me is an ethical culture that gives the company a better shot at actual compliance. To my way of thinking, a company can't make it onto the "100 best" list unless leaders have created a culture of decencies in the workplace and toward employees. In other words, a company starts doing the right thing by treating people within the company with respect, appreciation, and decency.

SKEPTIC'S CHALLENGE

While conceding that these companies are perhaps "more ethical" and probably more attractive places for employees to work than others, a skeptic might still ask what a culture of decencies does for investors. Do companies experience measurable returns for their investment in culture? Stated another way, can investors expect to derive an advantage from investing in companies that earn top scores on the Great Place to Work Institute survey?

In fact, investors do derive an advantage. Stocks of the public companies on *Fortune* magazine's "100 Best Companies to Work For" list produced more than three times the gains of the broad market over the last seven years, according to a study released by Russell Investment Group and the Great Place to Work Institute. The study suggests a strong link between workplace culture and a business's financial performance. "Great workplaces have significant competitive advantages as a result of the high trust relationships between employees and management," says Lyman. "Trust can contribute to higher levels of cooperation, greater commitment, lower employee turnover, decreased use of sick time, and improved customer support. These qualities translate into financial gains because the companies have lower voluntary turnover than their peers, are able to recruit the best employees to fit their culture and needs, provide top quality customer service and create innovative products and services," she adds.

CREATING GREAT WORKPLACES AND FINDING THE BEST

Creating environments that employees describe as "a great place to work" and in which employees are free to speak their minds relies on the practice of decencies on a regular basis by everyone in the organization. It also takes leadership at the top to start the process, reinforce the efforts along the way, and communicate the long-term benefits of creating and sustaining an organization culture based on trust. These practices go beyond the leaders at the top to become common acts among people throughout the organization. "That's what we find in the Best Companies that make our lists—a deep expression of the workplace culture in the actions of people throughout the organization," Lyman notes.

Most of the companies on the list demonstrate over-the-top generosity in good times as well as bad times. Yahoo!, for example, provides employees with subsidized on-site massages, haircuts, dentistry, car washes, and oil changes, not to mention stock options for all. Google, known for lavish employee benefits, operates free buses to shuttle employees living in San Francisco to its headquarters 33 miles south in Mountain View. The bus benefits employees and is good for the environment, which squares with Google's slogan of "Don't be evil." But there's a business purpose to what it does too. The vehicles have wireless Internet capability so passengers can work during the trip.

Google, like many other high-tech firms, offers a wealth of services for employees. Google offers the 1,000 workers at its headquarters free lunches and dinners cooked by a gourmet chef. The dinner is popular with Google's young engineers, who tend to be single and work late. Google also offers dry-cleaning services, washers and dryers for those who want to do their laundry during work, yoga and other fitness classes, and massages. Employees can get haircuts from visiting stylists, just as their cars can get washed or detailed by mobile car-wash businesses that visit Silicon Valley campuses. Again, it's all about giving employees what they want, eliminating distractions, and making it easier for employees to keep working.

Other forms of generosity are as numerous as the companies surveyed. Some of the more common gestures take the following forms:

- Part-time workers granted stock options
- Reimbursement for adoption expenses and fertility treatments
- Generous tuition reimbursement
- Subsidized child care

While all these benefits are welcome, not all of them qualify as decencies within the framework of this book. For these we have to drill deeper. When we do, we begin to see the common threads of smaller decencies within the leadership of the winning organizations. Leaders demonstrate willingness to share the limelight, a lack of executive pomposity, the propensity to give away credit and hoard blame, an interest in catching people doing things right, and, most important, integrity.

When we scrutinize some of the companies with the top scores, it's pretty easy to tease out the creative commitments they make to cultural well-being. We see supervisors who are not afraid to roll up their sleeves and take on the jobs of rank-and-file workers; employees—not just bosses—interviewing job applicants; open question-and-answer forums with honest answers; selflessness in community service; spot discretionary rewards; and more. These small decencies and others like them are ubiquitous within the population of Great Place to Work winners. Small decencies are often married with bigger decencies which have a programmatic, permanent nature but still arise out of the same values. Let's take a closer look at some of these companies.

Wegmans Food Markets

Business sector: Grocery chain
Number of employees: 31,800
Ownership: Private
Decency: Caring for customers and employees alike

Wegmans Food Markets has risen to the top of the Great Place to Work Institute list. Wegmans is a privately held Rochester, New York–based food market chain of over 70 locations and 31,800 employees. It was the number two great place to work on the *Fortune* list in 2006 and number three in 2007. In a field of contestants in which differentiation in cultural excellence proves difficult, Wegmans made a difference with its stories of culturally sensitive decencies, large and small. I had heard so much about the pervasiveness of decencies at Wegmans Food Markets that I wanted to experience the company for myself. I took a trip to its showcase store complex, where I spent a day talking to executives and hourly workers alike. I ate in the restaurant, explored the market, and sat down and talked to employees.

President Danny Wegman has often stated that the company's commitment to maintaining a great environment for employees delivers clear financial benefits and is a permanent part of its business strategy. I certainly witnessed a workplace with energized, personable employees taking care of details and customers. At Wegmans, employees are empowered to provide incredible service and to go above and beyond for customers. An employee shared this information about a coworker:

> Sally Jones [not her real name], at one of our Buffalo, New York, stores, had a regular customer who was in a wheelchair. Every week, the customer asked for Sally because of her caring nature. The customer came in one day with his wife and shared that he had been diagnosed with Alzheimer's. He has since been admitted to a nursing home and thus cannot come to Wegmans whenever he chooses. Sally explained how touched she was to have gotten to know her customer so well that he confided in her how his life had now changed forever. She found out from his wife that one day he was planning to come to the store to shop with her. Sally was excited because she knows that all he ever asks to do when he is able to go out of the nursing home is to go to Wegmans. Sally decided to brighten his day by getting him a thoughtful card and can of his favorite peanuts as a little way of saying, "We care and are thinking of you." I have always been proud of the way Sally cares

about people, but today I was really reminded of why I chose Wegmans as my place of employment.

Wegmans doesn't stop at caring for customers. It has a firm commitment to help employees as well. Caring for employees sometimes means helping them with needs outside of work. This is a difficult area some companies overlook. Not so at Wegmans. Case in point: Wegmans has established a fund called the Spirit of Giving to help employees in need with special circumstances. Recently, for example, a Wegmans store manager wrote a letter of thanks to the late Robert Wegman after Spirit of Giving money helped an employee at his store. This is the letter:

> It came to my attention that one of our employees has been without power in her home for quite a while. This particular individual lives alone in a trailer and has been unable to pay her gas and electric payments on her own. If she didn't work for Wegmans, I am sure that she would be without power for the unforeseen future. Late last night her power was restored. She told me this morning how nice it was to be warm and that when she awoke she didn't have to light a candle to see. Her gratitude is beyond my ability to explain. So there you have someone whom you may never have touched with your hand, but who has now been touched by your heart. On behalf of [said employee], I want to say "Thank you."

Another example of caring occurred in January 2006. A Wegmans employee was diagnosed with amyotrophic lateral sclerosis (ALS), also called Lou Gehrig's disease. ALS is a progressive neuromuscular disease that weakens and eventually destroys motor neurons (components of the nervous system that connect the brain with the skeletal muscles). There is no cure.

The employee has a love of sports. As a special gift, the corporate office along with his store was able to present him with a trip to the NCAA final four basketball tournament in Indianapolis for himself, his wife, and his two children. The company paid for everything—the airplane tickets, hotel accommodations, rental car, game admission, and food. The employee was also given $1,000 spending money, and the family was invited to attend luncheons featuring Dick Vitale and Bill Walton. The employee was elated and said, "I feel like a kid at Christmas."

In a March 28, 2006, article in the *Democrat and Chronicle*, the local newspaper in Rochester, New York, the employee was quoted as saying: "There's a reason why Wegmans was rated the No. 1 company in America to work for. They truly do care about their people. That they would do something like that at a time like this blows me away. There's my church, my family, and the people at Wegmans," he said. "That's how passionately I feel about my coworkers, my boss and this company. What they've done for me is truly a blessing."

Lest you think that story a one-off, consider this one. An employee who works in one of Wegmans' restaurants was recently diagnosed with cancer and had been out of work for a while. He was going through treatment, which made him extremely weak. When he came in to do shopping, he always used the motorized shopping carts Wegmans provides for this purpose. Just doing this small task exhausted him, and sometimes he could not even finish his shopping. The next time this employee needed to do some shopping, he called the store and had asked if there was some way they could put a few items together for him to pick up. A service desk manager quickly volunteered to shop for the groceries and deliver them to the employee's house. When she got back, she told the store manager that when she went to put away the groceries, she noticed that the refrigerator and the food storage shelves were almost empty. She was very upset about this and asked if the store could put a basket of food together. If necessary, she said, she would pay for it all. The basket was put together, paid for by the store, and taken to the employee. Since then, this service desk manager has continued to shop for the employee, learning what kinds of food he likes and what he was able to eat. This employee clearly models Wegmans' values of "make a difference, empowerment, respect, care, and high standards." But most importantly, she has made a difference to the employee in need.

WINNING INITIATIVES

Like Wegmans, every company earning a place on the "100 Best" list invests in its people and its workplace. Here are a few other initiatives that demonstrate the role of decencies in creating effective and productive work environments.

Principal Financial Group

Business sector: Financial services and insurance
Number of employees: 12,700
Ownership: Public
Decency: The Big Map of Initiatives

Principal Financial Group (PFG) uses the Big Map of Initiatives during new employee orientation to help everyone understand his or her role in the firm's success from the first day on the job. It is also provided to leaders for use with their teams.

The Big Map of Initiatives is a visual aid designed to give employees a snapshot of both what the company is doing and how it is being done. The map shows the flow of the major initiatives employees hear about throughout the year and covers the organization's purpose and mission, the success measures used for different initiatives, and how employees contribute to success through their work and upholding of the company's values. The map provides leaders and managers with a tool for reinforcing the message about each employees' importance in creating and sustaining the organization's business and culture. I see the map as a decency because it demonstrates that management values the work of each employee as a piece of the big picture.

Genentech

Business sector: Biotechnology and pharmaceuticals
Number of employees: 8,100
Ownership: Public
Decency: Office hours and dialogue days

Genentech has created a culture that supports intense curiosity. This culture is fueled by many programs and practices built into the structure of people's work lives. Yet the cultural practices of open questioning, honest conversations—no hierarchy, no buzzwords—are reflected in small practices and cultural decencies that have helped to elevate Genentech above its competitors.

Genentech has taken a cue from academia, where professors publicize office hours when they are available to students. At Genentech, as we noted in Chapter 7, every member of the Leadership Team is available for "office hours" once a month. Office hours give employees in various departments the opportunity for valuable informal one-on-one discussions on any topic. "It's a great opportunity to hear from employees who might not set up an official meeting but want to get your input on a project, voice a concern, or briefly get advice about managing an issue. It gives me the chance to hear what's on people's minds, which is valuable to hear as our department grows and matures," says Associate Director Margaret Pometta.

The Leadership Team office hours are part of the department's Dialogue Days program, a kind of "lunch and learn" at the department level, where employees have the chance to have lunch (or sometimes breakfast) and converse in small groups with leaders of the organization. Dialogue Days are held every Wednesday and are always well-attended.

Analytical Graphics, Inc.

Business sector: Information technology software
Number of employees: 251
Ownership: Private
Decency: Welcoming children into the workplace

Analytical Graphics, Inc. (AGI), understands that there are times when employees' children can't wait until a parent gets home. When that happens, the children are invited to spend time with the parent at the office. These office visits may be to see the mother or father after she or he has been away on business and the family needs to be reunited. Children frequently visit parents during Friday lunch/storytime sessions.

Additionally, emergency school closings, sick-day care, and change in day-care arrangements that may normally take an employee away from the office are not issues at AGI. AGI offers a variety of accommodations for AGI children: a private room for movie watching, a room with computers for games, even sitting next to the parent during the day. The children get a seemingly endless supply of healthy snacks and AGIers to dote on them.

American Speech-Language-Hearing Association

Business sector: Professional services
Number of employees: 219
Ownership: Not-for-profit
Decency: Effective recognition

At the American Speech-Language-Hearing Association, a small but effective Rockville, Maryland–based organization, staff members are encouraged to recognize the special efforts and accomplishments of their colleagues.

The company's rewards and recognition policy encourages people to keep the following principles in mind. This list, by the way, itemizes small decencies:

- *Be specific:* It gives the feedback power and impact.
- *Be individual:* When rewarding a team for a job well done, recognize individual efforts that allowed the team to succeed.

- *Be personal:* Each of us appreciates praise in a different way.
- *Be timely:* Give praise along the way; do not wait until the end of the year.
- *Be proportional:* Make the size of the acknowledgment commensurate with the project or deed being recognized.
- *Be sincere*

Banco Popular

Business sector: Financial services
Number of employees: 11,400
Ownership: Public
Decency: Employee college scholarship program

While serving as the president of Banco Popular, a financial services firm founded in Puerto Rico in 1893, CEO Rafael Carrión, Jr., recognized the importance of providing the opportunity of a college education to employees' children. To help make that dream come true, "don Papi," as Mr. Carrión, Jr., was known throughout Popular, created and personally funded an educational scholarship fund for the children of Popular employees. Today, this fund is known as the Rafael Carrión, Jr., Scholarship Fund, and all employees of all Popular companies in both Puerto Rico and the United States are eligible to apply for scholarships through this program. Since the fund's creation in 1992, a total of $1,695,100 has been distributed to 1,171 students.

Bright Horizons Family Solutions

Business sector: Education and training

Number of employees: 13,600
Ownership: Public
Decency: HEART toolkit

The goal of Bright Horizons Family Solutions is to become the world's biggest little company, according to CEO David Lissy. Bright Horizons Family Solutions is the world's leading provider of employer-sponsored child care, early education, and work/life solutions. Based in Watertown, Massachusetts, the company develops employer-sponsored child-care and early education programs and helps companies implement work/life strategies. Guided by its HEART principles of honesty, excellence, accountability, respect, and teamwork, Bright Horizons attracts people who like to work in a fun environment that celebrates the unique contributions of each individual.

A HEART toolkit (a package of training and communication materials) helps managers at each location continually reinforce the HEART mission, vision, and values. It helps them reinforce the HEART principles in a fun, interactive way. Gift giving is part of the Bright Horizons culture. Small tokens of appreciation are freely given to those who give so much of themselves each day. During the annual leadership conference, packages of HEART note cards are distributed to all attendees. The specially designed note cards feature heart-themed photographs on the front, and excerpts from the HEART principles on the back. While the cards are a nice gesture, I am more impressed by the decency of empowering site managers to instill the corporate values and arming them with a specially designed tool for this purpose. Giving site managers a head start in this process recognizes how busy their jobs are.

11

Five CEOs
Who Get It

There is properly no history, only biography.

RALPH WALDO EMERSON

The history of business is replete with examples of influential men and women. Some of these business leaders have acted out of stewardship, vision, and sacrifice. Others have acted out of opportunism, self-interest, and even criminality. Regardless of the leadership style in place, regardless of the industry, size, location, or success of the organization, someone is setting the behavioral examples. People are on the lookout for the little, genuine things that reflect well on the posted conduct codes, values lists, and HR policies. We hope to see alignment between the leader's conduct and the stated values of the organization. That will resonate with people. Of course, if they see the opposite; if followers perceive disconnect and hypocrisy, that will resonate with them too.

It's a pattern of small decencies that, repeated often enough, become a way of life or, as sociologists put it, "norms of reciprocity." At the minimum, these gestures, in ways large and small, will change a corporate culture for the better. Collectively small decencies can become the antidote to cultural decay. These are decencies that are beyond CSR and expressions of emotional intelligence. More related to *moral intelligence*, these are the acts that challenge the cynicism of employees. These are the decencies that follow the criteria I describe in Chapter 1: actionable, tangible, pragmatic, affordable, replicable, portable, and sustainable.

Organizations, just like civilizations, extend their cultures by modeling customs and behaviors to subsequent generations and leaders. This is called *tradition*. These behaviors become so entrenched and ubiquitous that few leaders would dare to challenge them. They become part of the fabric. Their sustainability ultimately depends on the value these decencies are perceived to have.

More frequently than not, the inspiration for these decencies emanates from an individual who by his or her character changes the course of the organization for the better. This chapter celebrates five such individuals.

1. REUBEN MARK, CHAIRMAN AND CEO, COLGATE–PALMOLIVE

Reuben Mark and I were classmates and fraternity brothers at Middlebury College. Fast forward 40-plus years. Today Reuben is revered for having personally led the transformation of a mid-sized, conservative consumer products company that had a primarily one-product identity—toothpaste—into a world-class, multiproduct global player.

In the 1990s when the stock market was rocking, Reuben was one of the few American CEOs to emphasize the importance of corporate culture on responsible governance. After the Colgate board of directors was honored by GovernanceMetrics International (only 17 of 1,600 companies studied were so recognized), the CEO of an independent research firm said, "After almost three years of stories of powerful leaders violating standards of ethics, Mark is an example of a CEO doing a good job."

Reuben Mark has been a living example of the fact that humility and cultural sensitivity are not inconsistent with operational strength and success. Sheila Wellington, former president of the women's advocacy group Catalyst, recalls bumping into him one evening on the street in Manhattan. He looked anything but the CEO in his weather-beaten parka. "He wants his company to be the superstar, not him," she says. He is historically press-shy. He is as comfortable with Colgate's factory workers as he is with Wall Street analysts. During a trip in the 1990s to the company's facilities in Mexico City, he disarmed nervous employees by joking in fluent Spanish. A results-oriented leader, he even declined an interview with a publication honoring him as a finalist for CEO of the year. He believes it offensive for one person to take credit for the efforts of an entire organization. Ric Marshall, chief analyst of The Corporate Library, an independent research firm, put it this way: "Mark stands out precisely because he does not stand out. That's what a CEO is supposed to do: quietly build value for shareholders without ostentation. These are the people who keep the market going."

As we saw in Chapter 9, Reuben Mark's interest in improving education is legendary. Under his direction, Colgate adopted a poverty-stricken New York City school that had become totally dysfunctional. The company sponsored the school's rehabilitation, advised on the selection of new management, and helped restructure the curriculum. Colgate employees sat on the school's advisory board and helped in the management, budget, and operations of the school. "I was stunned to see how kids were being treated—they were essentially warehoused until they turned 16 or dropped out," Reuben told *Chief Executive* magazine. "The most important thing Colgate contributed was not money but people. This was not a classic adopt-a-school project in which we write a check and the school spends it. If I as a CEO had not been involved in the beginning, my people would not have felt free to spend their time or energy on the project and allowed to take time off work to get involved."

After college, I had lost track of Reuben until the mid-1980s when I discovered he had just been made CEO of his company. When we reconnected, I asked Reuben if he could identify the one thing about himself that he considered the primary factor in his success. "That's easy," he told me. "I have made it my business during my tenure in various management roles to make absolutely sure that nothing important or creative at Colgate-Palmolive is perceived as my idea."

In the 2004 book *The Transparent Leader*, Herb Baum wrote the following:

> Shortly after my appointment as the new CEO of Dial, I received a phone call while I was in London on vacation from Reuben Mark, the chairman and CEO of Colgate-Palmolive, a major competitor. Colgate competes directly with Dial in several market segments and often comes out on top. I have a lot of respect for the company, and I knew Reuben to be an outstanding CEO with an excellent reputation. The day he called, he said that he had in his possession a CD containing Dial's marketing plan for the year. It

had been given to him by a member of his sales force (a former Dial employee who had taken it with him when he left to join Colgate), and it meant that one of Dial's most important product line's strategies had been revealed, and could result in the loss of revenue, profits, and market share.

"Herb," Reuben said, "one of our new salespeople gave this CD to one of my sales managers. I'm not going to look at this information, and I'm sending it back to you right now. I'll handle it on this end."

It was the clearest case of leading with honor and transparency I've witnessed in my career. After all, who expects a CEO to call his competitor and tell him they have a copy of their detailed business strategy? If he hadn't, I never would have known, but that one call gave me more insight into his character than anything else. It wasn't hard to see why he had been so successful in his career. He knew he didn't need to gain an unfair competitive advantage to succeed, even when he was presented with the opportunity. He chose not to abandon his leadership style, and he had the courage to stick to his principles even when it meant giving up confidential information that could have helped his company gain an edge. Transparency takes courage.

2. F. KENNETH IVERSON, CEO OF NUCOR

From the 1960s through the 1990s when the U.S. steel industry was struggling to be profitable, Nucor consistently made profits. Much of this success is attributed to the late Ken Iverson (he died in April 2002). As a young man growing up in a Chicago suburb, Iverson learned to respect those who worked with their hands as well as their heads. A degreed engineer from Cornell, Ken Iverson earned his master's degree in metallurgy at Purdue University.

Iverson joined Nucor (formerly Nuclear Corporation of America) in 1962. It had been unwieldy and unprofitable and had a history of mediocrity. His transformation of Nucor was in no small way a result of innovative and courageous human resources practices. Employee turnover was about 1 to 5 percent a year, compared to the 25 percent turnover typical at other steel companies. Rather than lay off employees, Nucor shortened its workweek when demand dropped.

As had Reuben Mark, Ken Iverson credited his employees with most of the productivity improvements. All levels of employees, not just management, were on an incentive compensation system. He eliminated the counterproductive status symbols commonly found in other steel companies. He did away with assigned parking spaces and company cars. All Nucor executives had to eat in the company cafeteria with all the other workers. Throughout his 30-year tenure, the corporate headquarters consisted of a rented suite of offices in the same building Nucor occupied in 1966.

Nucor executives received no benefits except those that the hourly workers were entitled to as well. On business trips, everyone flew coach class. Any hourly worker who had a problem with a manager could take the complaint directly to Iverson. Iverson answered his own phone, responded to all employee questions within 24 hours, and, as noted in Chapter 9, insisted that all employees be listed in each year's annual report on its cover in alphabetical order.

Sometimes his determination to eliminate differences between management and workers went too far. When he became CEO, he challenged the tradition of different colored hard hats, which had become status symbols that widened the divide between functional areas. His vision of leadership stemmed from a belief that the authority of people didn't come from the color of the hat they wore. He insisted that henceforth all hard hats would be green.

As it turned out, this decision had unintended consequences. Its top-down quality contradicted another of his values—employee involvement. It was critical for workers, for example, to distinguish quickly between operations people and maintenance workers. In an emergency, you have to be able to spot the maintenance workers immediately. So Iverson admitted his mistake and changed the policy. Today, everyone wears green hard hats except for maintenance people, who wear yellow, and visitors, who wear white.

Iverson believed in minimizing layers of management, treating people as equals, turning everyone into decision makers, and encouraging innovation. He believed that employees, not managers, are the engines of progress. To Iverson, a manager exists only, "To help the people you manage accomplish extraordinary things." He was an early advocate of giving employees a stake in the business and was an early proponent of empowerment. He allowed his division managers to decide "where the locus of decision-making power should reside."

Iverson's contract with employees was based on four clear-cut principles.

1. Management is obligated to manage the company in such a way that employees will have the opportunity to earn according to their productivity.

2. Employees should feel confident that if they do their jobs properly, they will have a job tomorrow.
3. Employees have the right to be treated fairly and must believe that they will be.
4. Employees must have an avenue of appeal when they believe they are being treated unfairly.

Iverson was amazingly accessible, and not just to employees. Chip Joyce was a college student in 1991. His history professor had often referred to Ken Iverson's corporate leadership, so on a whim Chip drove to Nucor's Charlotte, North Carolina, headquarters. The receptionist welcomed him warmly and gave him some brochures. She sensed the student wanted something more, so she said, "Do you want to meet Ken? Hold on . . ." A minute later he was in Iverson's office. I'll let Joyce finish the story:

Mr. Iverson was a strapping man who exuded confidence and ability. He was in a suit that he wore well, but he could easily have been in dungarees and a hard hat. He was in his mid-sixties, evidenced by his wrinkles, but contradicted by his obvious physical strength and energy of a thirty-year-old. Most striking, though, were his blue eyes, which were those of a man who was at ease in the universe—that's how I can best describe it.

3. DOUGLAS R. CONANT, CEO, CAMPBELL SOUP COMPANY

As another model of understated and unpretentious class, Doug Conant has made a clear footprint among success stories in corporate life.

After getting a degree in marketing, Conant's career included successful assignments at Parker Brothers, the maker of "Monopoly." When General Mills decided to sell off its toy and game business, his job was unceremoniously eliminated, and he was told to clear out his office by lunchtime. At his next job, Nabisco Foods Company, he earned a reputation as a skillful marketer of timeworn brands, helping to revive the market share for Planter's nuts and Lifesavers candy.

Despite its iconic status, Campbell Soup found itself struggling in the 1990s with softening sales and intense competition. Some analysts predicted that the fiercely independent 140-year-old company might become a takeover candidate. Conant arrived at Campbell Soup in 2001. His first steps were to innovate product development, revitalizing sales by introducing soups that were attractive to contemporary, on-the-run consumers. In the process, he boosted employee morale; upgraded tired plants, products, and images; and acquired several European dry soup brands. The business press was concerned whether the "mild-mannered executive" had the right stuff to be the "revolutionary" he needed to be to turn Campbell around.

Yet another low-keyed executive at a time when celebrity CEOs were in vogue, Conant was a natural. Jim Collins, author of *Good to Great,* believes that great executives are seemingly genetically different: they exude humility and do not think that business ethics is an oxymoron. Richard Cavanagh, president and CEO of the Conference Board, calls leaders such as Conant "level-five" executives. "Their ambitions are not for themselves but the institutions they serve."

In one presentation, Conant characterized himself as "an introvert who can't play golf." To his credit, as a young executive, similar to Reuben Mark, he was accessible to everyone, took on menial tasks, and made it his business to know the job from the worker's perspective. He openly lets everyone know that he retains an executive coach and insists that he has the good fortune of being surrounded by a team full of coaches, referring to his colleagues. He holds casual company cafeteria gatherings to report on Campbell's performance. These have expanded to include employees from locations outside the United States by teleconference.

Learning the power of "thank you" during his post-Parker job search, Conant regularly wrote thank you notes within 24 hours of a job interview. He's been writing notes—thousands each year—ever since. Conant encourages his people to inform him of achievements and promotions, as well as personal losses, sicknesses, and small kindnesses. At Nabisco, Conant wrote 5 to 10 personal notes *every day* to employees and others recognizing these experiences. Today, at Campbell offices around the world, it is common to see framed notes from the CEO on cubical and office walls. It's about "Doug's natural warmth and interest in people," says Mitch Wienick, a Pennsylvania executive coach. "The notes are another way to reach out not physically, but to psychically touch someone."

4. HERB BAUM, FORMER CEO, THE DIAL CORPORATION

Through his years at Hasbro, Quaker State Corporation, and The Dial Corporation, Herb Baum left his mark as not only a turnaround CEO but also as a leader who successfully revitalized corporate cultures. A passionate advocate of integrity and decency, and an acknowledged laureate of transparency in the corporate setting, Baum was the right leader at the right time for Dial. The last days of the tenures of his predecessors, John Teets and Malcolm Jozoff, were not impressive. In both cases, sales were slipping, earnings estimates were missed, and employees described the atmosphere in the company as less than motivating. The company's leadership was far more opaque than transparent in its dealings outside and within the enterprise. Even the board of directors had been kept in the dark as to the developing storm clouds.

The board ultimately acted in August 2000. Jozoff resigned, and Herb Baum was put at the helm. By the time of its sale to the German company Beiersdorf AG in 2003, the darker days had become a distant memory. Sales growth, higher margins, and an improved balance sheet were among the accomplishments during Herb's tenure. His commitment to corporate responsibility and community service has become part of the cultural fabric at Dial.

Herb Baum was a tireless advocate of openness and accessibility. In his book *The Transparent Leader*, Baum says, "The road to transparency is itself an open one—it's not a traffic jam with corporate politics . . . I stress actual physical accessibility as a tool to develop our culture."

One way he became accessible was through a program called "Hotdogs with Herb." He describes this as "a fun, casual lunch where I get to spend quality time with a small group of employees . . . It allows them to get to know me, and gives me a chance to get to know them and listen to their concerns or feedback . . . We always have hotdogs—my favorite dish . . . It's a small thing, but it gives employees a chance to understand how I think about things . . . There's no agenda; we just sit around and talk about things from office amenities to our products to where the best place in town for pizza is! It's also great for corporate culture because it's real, down-to-earth, ongoing communication, and it helps me discern fact from fiction. If there's a rumor, it can be squashed right away before it has a chance to infect the company. People can ask me whatever they want during the Hotdogs with Herb sessions. They will get a straight answer. We solve problems, change policies, and get to know each other, and in the process I work to be a good accessible leader, a friend, and hopefully even a mentor."

5. HERB KELLEHER, CHAIRMAN AND CEO, SOUTHWEST AIRLINES

In his endorsement of the 1996 book *Nuts!*, the story of Southwest Airlines by Jackie and Kevin Freiberg, leadership guru Warren Bennis calls the Southwest story, "A blueprint for all organizations that want to succeed—not just airlines." Noted Harvard professor and author Rosabeth Moss Kanter refers to the story as, "An inspiring tale of remarkable results possible when employees are liberated to take charge of the rules and have fun on the job . . . It offers valuable lessons about leadership and profitability to all that care about the future of their companies."

The Freibergs characterize Kelleher, a pioneer in employee empowerment, as, "Always the first to give Southwest's employees credit for the company's tremendous success. The stories of Kelleher's down-to-earth approach, boundless energy, egalitarianism, unpretentiousness and decency are almost endless." The business results from the upstart airline have been consistently profitable since 1973. Southwest Airlines has, by most measures, outperformed the entire industry.

Fun, celebrations, and almost antiestablishment behavior, while being the Kelleher legacy, pale in the face of his instinct for decency. Among his commandments is this: "Be humble: success is hardly ever your own doing and rarely irreversible." Southwest's HR department is called "The People Department." The airline's mantra is, "Treat everyone with kindness and equal respect; you never know who you are talking to." It even publishes a corporate newsletter called *Luv Lines.*

Kelleher's philosophy is that, "Failure is not fatal." Southwest does all that it can to maintain the dignity of and respect for employees who make mistakes. He felt that the costs of getting burned once in a while are insignificant compared to the benefits of people feeling free to take risks and be creative.

Kelleher believes that, "Culture is one of the most precious things a company has, so you must work harder at it than anything else. In any organization, culture is the present manifestation of the past: the challenges, successes, mistakes, and lessons learned. Culture becomes the organization's memories; it guides and provides a sense of dignity, stability, and organizational boundaries. The central components include family, fun, love, individuality, egalitarianism and altruism." He believes that "employees are number one. The way you treat your employees is the way they will treat your customers."

Kelleher's expressions of decency are the stuff of myth, from the personal intimacy (when he was president, an employee couldn't have a birth or death in the family without hearing from him) to the outrageous. Many people still remember the arm-wrestling showdown between Kelleher and the CEO of Stevens Aviation in 1992. Both Stevens and Southwest had claimed the exclusive right to use the tagline "Plane Smart" in their advertising. Instead of suing each other and letting the matter drag out in the courts, Kelleher suggested an arm-wrestling competition with the winner keeping the rights to the slogan. And Kelleher is an attorney! Kelleher lost the battle but won the war. The event generated so much goodwill and publicity for both airlines that Stevens let Southwest continue using the tagline.

Kelleher created a "culture committee" to honor Southwest's "unsung heroes"—people behind the scenes in less glamorous jobs. Each year one of these is selected to be the "Hero of the Heart" for his or her efforts in supporting the Southwest agenda. The maintenance people are recognized and celebrated through the "Top Wrench" program to reward the efforts of mechanics who might otherwise go unrecognized. And to acknowledge the efforts of the cleaning people, the company initiated a "Top Cleaner" program. *Nuts!* summarizes Southwest's philosophy as a combination of decencies, including:

- Say "thank you" often
- Always celebrate people from the heart
- Make heroes and heroines of employees who glorify your company's values
- Find people who serve behind the scenes and celebrate their contributions

Typical of the thread of decency that runs through Southwest, the Freibergs report the time several years ago that Colleen Barrett, then serving as chief people officer, noticed that a long-tenure employee seemed suddenly to be having problems and receiving complaints. When confronted, the employee started to cry and went on to describe her difficult divorce, a custody battle over her three-year-old son, and an $1,800 debt for legal fees.

After consoling the employee, Barrett delivered an envelope with $1,800 in cash from her own personal account. The employee was overwhelmed and continues to contribute to the company in ever-expanding roles. (Colleen Barrett is now president of the company, a signal of how much the Southwest Airlines culture values her type of leadership.)

Kelleher inspired the company to create the "Home for the Holidays" program. Every winter holiday season, the company donates tickets to senior citizens so they can fly home to see their relatives. In 1996 alone, Southwest flew 850 seniors to visit their families during the Home-for-the-Holidays promotion. Thousands of individuals have experienced the same opportunity over the years, and in two of those years Southwest was cited by the president of the United States for this program. As for transparency, the company believes that the more employees know, the more they care. The leadership is known for saturating people with information.

Frequently cited as a model of collaborative leadership, Southwest Airlines believes that when people are committed, they are bound emotionally or intellectually to a purpose. "Compliant people simply go through the motions and put in their time; they have no emotional or spiritual attachment to the cause their work represents. Commitment doesn't come with position and it can't be bought. Commitment must be earned," Freiberg notes.

12

Your Turn: Putting Small Decencies into Action

We should trust ourselves to be both great and good,
and if sometimes that trust is misplaced, more often
it will be merited, for there is that within all of us which
cries out for a better and fairer world.

CHARLES HANDY, *THE HUNGRY SPIRIT*

When you have a father who was a psychiatrist and a wife who is a psychologist, nothing appears linear to you. Things for me don't have simply a beginning, a middle, and an end. I quickly leave the main path for side roads, shortcuts that are anything but, and dead ends that lead to new beginnings. Most disciplines and functions in business exist for me in three dimensions.

Case in point: The sales process for me is not simply a linear process of prospecting, presenting, and closing. What I love best is the eccentric style displayed by great salespeople. I'm fascinated by them. While they are essential members of the team, they are frequently frustrating to manage. Yet if their eccentricity is effective, how do you recruit for it?

Eccentricity pervades creative and innovative people in every organization. It's no accident that Silicon Valley is located in

California, the state with perhaps the highest threshold for eccentricity. I care about eccentricity not because I've found answers or discovered the essential DNA for it, but because I've come to believe that managing eccentric talent and coaching a culture to be tolerant of these potentially productive or creative people will pay dividends. Making a place for eccentricity is an important element of good leadership . . . decent leadership.

Effective leadership has to make a place for ethics too. Ethics, like eccentricity, can't easily fit in neat little boxes. For me, there was always more to compliance than the formulaic programs promulgated by federal regulations. While we've learned to walk around with our SOX on (pun intended), we also have to live within corporate cultures that are sometimes messy and always amorphous. At the same time we need to experience a culture that is enabling enough to reconcile the post-Enron legal heavy-handedness with the virtues of a healthy corporate culture: non-threatening, open, motivating, and flexible. Flexible enough not only to tolerate eccentricity, but to value it.

Many organizations perceive small decencies as the eccentricities of top performers. Just as eccentric salespeople deliver great results in the field, small decencies deliver great benefits to the organization. One key goal of this book is to suggest that small decencies are not just instrumental in forming corporate culture but are valuable in and of themselves, for their own sake. This view is still sufficiently eccentric for many corporate cultures to be afraid to fully embrace it.

Nevertheless, I hope that I've made a persuasive case that decency as a cultural imperative will produce short- and long-term benefits. Yet I'm realistic enough to acknowledge that some in the business community will want to calculate the payback of this approach to guiding a corporate culture. You know, "Show me the money!"

I suggest that small decencies cannot be evaluated like other investments. By definition, small decencies don't impose significant costs on the organization. They are essentially free, and they usually don't take a lot of time away from other activities. Under these circumstances, the idea of calculating an ROI for small decencies just doesn't compute.

But few organizations will draw clear lines between small, bigger, and big decencies. The return question is really about all kinds of decencies lumped together. I'll be honest. There haven't been specific studies about the payback of decencies as a whole. There are mixed results with the payback issue for bigger decencies: some companies compute a return on initiatives, others do not. To my mind, the best indication we have as to the monetary value of decency is the statistics amassed by the Great Place to Work Institute, which reinforce the link between decent cultures and stellar long-term financial results.

Working with the institute has shown me that the lever to financial results is going to be the impact of decencies on employee engagement. Our concerns have now returned to the talent shortage and the challenge of keeping our best performers engaged and productive. The estimates on the cost of employee turnover vary widely, but the direct costs are only the tip of the iceberg. The indirect costs on our work environment and organizational cultures are even harder to swallow. To my mind, what fuels the employee engagement challenge is the energy-depleting binge/purge, hire/fire, please go/please stay dynamics of the last 25 years.

I'm convinced that employees around the world desire to do work that matters in a culture that provides meaning. They want work that is less transactional, more transformational, and, occasionally, inspirational. They want their jobs to sustain enough idealism, intimacy, and depth so that they can act on their vision of creating a better world for their families and communities.

Theresa M. Welbourne, CEO of eePulse, Inc., says that, "Simply valuing employees is not enough." Her research has shown that there is a precious balance between valuing people and creating an optimal sense of urgency that inspires workers to work toward the goals of the organization. Since 1996, Welbourne has been gathering data continuously from organizations worldwide. She focuses on the energy level of employees. Her work shows that employee energy predicts important business measures such as employee turnover, absenteeism, customer service, productivity, and more. "As a researcher in the HR field, I often started out by examining how large HR programs drive individual and organizational performance, but what I found out in the energy studies is that small, everyday behaviors can have the highest impact on driving results," she says.

"When companies engage in small decencies that positively affect employee energy, the result is that employees engage in similar decencies," she adds. "They help each other; they come up with new ideas and implement them; they work on teams even though it may take them away from their core jobs; and they help their companies by doing things that are good for the firm but not part of their everyday job."

The drumbeats around humility, civility, respect, ethical culture, and, in the words of futurist Patricia Aburdene, "conscious capitalism" have become increasingly loud and sustained. I come away with the unwavering belief that the role of decency in enriching a corporate culture has little to do with softness, submissiveness, or indecisiveness. Decency may be therapeutic, but it's not therapy. Nor is decency an impediment to competitiveness or business survival.

As always, it comes down to leadership. "A key task for a boss is to make it clear to everyone that a better form of leadership is happening," says my colleague Bob Lee. Leadership needs to be tangible and visible. Moral sensitivity, small decisions, thank yous, and hellos are the gestures that matter day-to-day. They are not manipulations. Commitment to cultural decency won't relieve every aspect of work-life stress and imbalance. But it can be a tonic to mitigate the most destructive aspects of our commercial dynamism. The option to manage by command and control is always present. But I argue that it is exactly the goodwill built up by decencies that allows the leader to enact the tough decisions that organizations need to make it through hard times.

Loud voices suggest that business can't afford the "extras" like decencies in hard times. "Business is a competitive sport for tough players—those who play it nice quite often fall behind," says Don Manvel, chairman and CEO of AVL North America, echoing a belief common to many CEOs. "In tough times you simply can't afford to take prisoners," Manvel says.

We can't blame CEOs for any resistance to decency because many corporate cultures are still ambivalent about it. And if from day to day we've seen businesspeople in the throes of indecency, we recognize their behavior as a dimension of humanity. At the same time, it really is our obligation to reject the notion that decencies may be nice but are luxuries, easily jettisoned when our belts must be tightened. Our willingness to be decent at work can't depend on whether business is up or down, or whether we are in a good mood or not, or whether it's raining.

Decencies don't amount to anything until we take the trouble to make them come alive through concrete action in all kinds of weather.

The world is struggling to emerge from a dark and trying period in the economy, a period characterized by Wall Street accounting scandals and CEO skulduggery. We've seen the face of business at its worst, and it hasn't been a pretty sight. We've seen similar issues in government and in religious and not-for-profit groups. It's time to rediscover the power of organizations at their best.

That's the purpose behind *The Manager's Book of Decencies*. Small gestures really are the beginning to building great organizations. It starts with individual acts performed by people who make a conscious decision about how they are going to behave.

Are you one of these people? Will you join me in this mission of extending small decencies throughout the world of work? Will you help build a community that talks about decencies and wrestles with how small decency is manifest in different regions of the world, in different kinds of organizations? We've launched a Web site, www.bookofdecencies.com, to celebrate small decencies. Please go there to share your thoughts; and better yet, share the examples of small decencies that have helped strengthen your corporate culture. There you will also find interesting material that for length reasons didn't make it into the book, links to related sites, and other resources.

I also hope you spread the message of small decencies. Let your friends, colleagues, and professional network know about this simple idea. You'll be helping to make organizations better places to do our life's calling. As a result, we will demonstrate to the world that decency may well be the most potent form of corporate social responsibility.

As Alan Kay, the visionary computer designer, so famously said, "The best way to predict the future is to invent it." Let's invent a better future together by applying small decencies wherever we happen to find ourselves. If you're like most successful leaders, you probably owe part of your success to having acted with decency. If you're like most focused, busy people, you probably could do more.

Endnotes

Chapter 1

5 *Organizations have a feel about them* . . . Charles Handy, *The Hungry Spirit: Beyond Capitalism—A Quest for Purpose in the Modern World* (New York: Broadway Books, 1999), 150.

6 *As I come in the door of a business for the first time,* . . . John Cowan, *Small Decencies: Reflections and Meditations on Being Human at Work* (New York: Harper Business, 1992), 17–18.

6 *Think of your children or cherished loved ones* . . . Ibid, 162.

7 *We will not change what's wrong with our culture* . . . The full text of Koppel's commencement remarks may be found at http://news-service .stanford.edu/news/1998/june17/koppel98.html.

8 *We find ourselves relating to a word that reflects specific behaviors* . . . The Dutch philosopher Erasmus (1466–1536) first used the word *decency* in its modern meaning of civility; decency not as a moral imperative, but as an obligation to be respectful to others.

16 *Consider a building with a few broken windows* . . . Malcolm Gladwell, *The Tipping Point: How Little Things Can Make a Big Difference* (Boston: Back Bay Books, 2002), 113.

Chapter 2

28 *Leadership is about values, not law* . . . Dov Seidman, Public Hearing Agenda and Written Testimony, United States Sentencing Commission, Thurgood Marshall Federal Judiciary Building, Washington, DC, March 17, 2004.

28 *Although the SEC can implement rules* . . . Cynthia Glassman, SEC Commissioner and Chairman, Stress Importance of Ethical Culture, *Federal Ethics Report*, Volume 10, Issue 4, published April 2003 by CCH Washington Service Bureau.

31 *Sometimes it's the smallest acts* . . . Joseph L. Badaracco, Jr., "A Lesson for the Times: Learning from Quiet Leaders," Ivey Management Services, January/February 2003, 4.

33 *Creating a New Employment Contract* . . . David Noer, "Creating a New Employment Contract," Noer Consulting, Greensboro, NC. Used by permission.

36 *There's no relaxing, no cruise control* . . . Robert B. Reich, *The Future of Success: Working and Living in the New Economy* (New York: Vantage Books, 2002), 222.

37 *Where will I find the inner strength* . . . Harold Kushner, *Living a Life That Matters* (New York: Anchor Books, 2002), 76.

Chapter 3

42 *Do [potential leaders] have the proper relationship* . . . Jim Collins, *Good to Great: Why Some Companies Make the Leap . . . and Others Don't* (New York: HarperCollins, 2001), 89.

43 *Courage is about making tough choices* . . . Jim Kouzes and Barry Posner, *A Leader's Legacy* (New York: Jossey-Bass, 2006), 139.

43 *Tom Peters believes that leaders must create new worlds* . . . Tom Peters, *Thriving on Chaos: Handbook for a Management Revolution*, Reprint Edition (New York: Harper Paperbacks, 1988), 216.

43 *An essential factor in leadership* . . . Warren Bennis and Burt Nanus, *Leaders: Strategies for Taking Charge* (New York: Collins Business Essentials, 2003), 14.

44 *Today's leaders have to be concerned about tomorrow's world* . . . Kouzes and Posner, *A Leader's Legacy*, 100.

44 *"When I'm through . . ."* Henry Ford's personal resistance to collaboration during most of his career does not diminish the force of his vision.

45 *In short, an essential factor* . . . Bennis and Nanus, *Leaders*, 98.

45 *Why does one inner city kid* . . . Kevin Cashman, *Leadership from the Inside Out* (New York: TCLG, 1998), 67.

46 *The third test is a willingness to engage* . . . This three-part test of integrity is necessary if we are to avoid a paradox. If integrity is merely aligning one's action with one's values, then Adolph Hitler and Josef Stalin had integrity. After all, they both acted on the basis of their deeply held beliefs. Where their integrity failed them was in their unwillingness to articulate their objectives (both insisted on secrecy), and they certainly were unwilling to have a dialogue on the matter.

48 *My decision to tell employees was never in doubt* . . . Amy Lyman, "Building Trust in the Workplace," Great Place to Work Institute. Available at http://resources.greatplacetowork.com/article/pdf/building_trust_in_the_workplace.pdf.

48 *I am prepared to relinquish control* . . . Reinhard K. Sprenger, *Trust: The Best Way to Manage* (London: Cyan Communications, 2004), 63.

49 *If you don't trust, then what?* . . . Kouzes and Posner, *A Leader's Legacy*, 75.

49 *If the ideas are merely proclaimed* . . . Peters, *Thriving on Chaos*, 211.

51 *One standard is worth a thousand* . . . Dale Dauten, *The Gifted Boss* (New York: William Morrow, 1999), 34.

52 *I was visiting a retail company* . . . Scott Cawood and Rita Bailey, *Destination Profit* (Mountain View, CA: Davies-Black Publishing, 2006), 14.

53 *How people are treated increasingly determines* . . . Ibid., 13.

54 *It is leadership that seeks to shape* . . . Terrence E. Deal and Allan A. Kennedy, *The New Corporate Cultures: Revitalizing the Workplace after Downsizing, Mergers, and Reengineering* (New York: Perseus Books, 2000), 37.

54 *In "A Recipe for Glue," he lists* . . . David Noer, *Breaking Free: A Prescription for Personal and Organizational Change* (New York: Jossey-Bass, 1996), 9. Used by permission.

55 *A Recipe for Glue* . . . Ibid.

Chapter 4

77 *I want you to take your extra 15 minutes* . . . Patricia Sellars, "How I Manage," *Fortune*, October 16, 2006.

Chapter 5

81 *They cared much more* . . . Cawood and Bailey, *Destination Profit*, 15.

82 *The talent war is over* . . . "The Search for Talent," *The Economist*, October 7–13, 2006, 4.

83 *Employees who receive that recognition* . . . Donna Deeprose, *How to Recognize and Reward Employees* (New York: American Management Association, 1994), vii.

83 *ASAP Cube* . . . Bob Nelson and Dean Spitzer, *The 1001 Rewards & Recognition Fieldbook: The Complete Guide* (New York: Workman Publishing, 2002).

87 *Peggy Noonan, a speechwriter for former President Ronald Reagan* . . . Peggy Noonan, *What I Learned in the Revolution: A Political Life in the Reagan Era* (New York: Random House, 2003), 67.

94 *Life's Little Instruction Book* . . . H. Jackson Brown, Jr., *Life's Little Instruction Book* (New York: Rutledge Hill Press, 1997).

Chapter 6

103 *This is the fifth of* . . . Stephen Covey, *The Seven Habits of Highly Successful People* (New York: Free Press, 2004). See Habit 5, 235–260.

Chapter 7

111 *Bethlehem Steel was losing market share* . . . John Strohmeyer, *Crisis in Bethlehem: Big Steel's Struggle to Survive* (Pittsburgh: University of Pittsburgh Press, 1994), 218.

111 *Imagine building three golf courses* . . . Ken Iverson, *Plain Talk: Lessons from a Business Maverick* (New York: Wiley & Sons, 1998), 55.

122 *Several factors, such as the nature of the apology* . . . Jennifer K. Robbennolt, "Apologies and Legal Settlement: An Empirical Examination," *Michigan Law Review*, Vol. 102, No. 460, 2003.

132 *An ailing organization can open itself* . . . Robert E. Hardy and Randy Schwartz, *The Self-Defeating Organization: How Smart Companies Can Stop Outsmarting Themselves* (New York: Addison-Wesley, 1996), 170.

133 *There were times that day* . . . Joseph Nocera, *A Piece of the Action: How the Middle Class Joined the Money Class* (New York: Touchstone Press, 1995), 312.

133 *On October 28, 1987* . . . Ibid.

Chapter 8

136 *In Japan, for example* . . . Japan has one of the highest suicide rates in the world. The number of people who killed themselves in 2005 rose from the previous year by 227 people to 32,552, according to National Police Agency figures. See "Overwork Pushed Japan Software Worker to Suicide," by Martyn Williams, IDG News Service, July 12, 2006.

137 *It is never over* . . . Noer, *Healing the Wounds: Overcoming the Trauma of Layoffs and Revitalizing Downsized Organizations* (San Francisco: Jossey-Bass, 1993), 109.

138 *Barnholt understood that the downsizing* . . . Daniel Roth, "How to Cut Pay, Lay Off 8,000 People, and Still Have Workers Who Love You. It's Easy: Just Follow the Agilent Way," *Fortune,* February 4, 2002.

145 *The workforce reduction notification* . . . "RadioShack Fires 400 Employees by E-mail," *BusinessWeek,* August 30, 2006.

147 *This word acknowledges* . . . Cawood and Bailey, *Destination Profit,* 198.

Chapter 9

167 *There is no evidence* . . . David Vogel, *The Market for Virtue: The Potential and Limits of Corporate Social Responsibility* (Washington, DC: Brookings Institution Press, 2005), 58.

169 *Corporations not only have citizens* . . . Handy, *The Hungry Spirit,* 157.

169 *Within months the absenteeism* . . . Ibid., 162.

Chapter 10

174 *Great workplaces have significant competitive* . . . Russell analysts compared the performance of a stock portfolio based on the "100 Best" list to the performance of the Russell 3000 Index (representing the broad U.S. equity market) and the S&P 500 (representing large-cap investments). The study found that the "100 Best" portfolio, adjusted annually to reflect changes to the list between 1998 and 2004, provided a cumulative return of 176 percent, compared with lesser gains of 42 percent for the Russell 3000 and 39 percent by the S&P 500. An initial investment of $1,000 on January 1, 1998, in publicly traded companies on the "100 Best" portfolio, adjusted annually, would have risen to $2,760.04, versus $1,415.62 for the Russell 3000 and $1,387.70 for the S&P 500, by December 31, 2004.

175 *That's what we find in the* . . . Amy Lyman in an interview with the author.

180 *There's a reason why Wegmans* . . . Scott Ptioniak, "Wegmans Treats Employee, Family to a Final Four Dream," *Democrat and Chronicle,* March 28, 2006, B1.

Chapter 11

189 *Mark stands out precisely* . . . "Colgate's Mark: Teaching Corporate Citizenship," *CBS MarketWatch,* September 18, 2003.

190 *I was stunned to see how kids* . . . "Finding What Really Works in Education," *Chief Executive*, May 1994, 48.

190 *Shortly after my appointment* . . . Herb Baum and Tammy Kling, *The Transparent Leader: How to Build a Great Company through Straight Talk, Openness, and Accountability* (New York: Collins, 2004), 31.

193 *To help the people you manage accomplish* . . . Tom Brown, "The Art of Keeping Management Simple," *Management Update*, Harvard Business School Publishing, May 1998.

193 *Management is obligated* . . . Ken Iverson, *Plain Talk: Lessons from a Business Maverick* (New York: Wiley & Sons, 1998), 21. Nucor's Commitment to Employees may also be found on the Nucor Web site at www.nucor.com/aboutus.htm.

194 *Mr. Iverson was a strapping man* . . . Chip Joyce, "Ken Iverson: Proof That Ayn Rand's Heroes Exist," *Capitalism Magazine*, April 2002.

195 *Their ambitions are not for themselves* . . . Daniel Cattau, "Souper CEO: Doug Conant, Campbell Soup's Top Executive, Is Heating Up Sales with His Insightful and Reflective Leadership," *Northwestern Magazine*, Spring 2005.

196 *It's about Doug's natural warmth* . . . Ibid.

197 *By the time of its sale* . . . Dial was acquired by Henken HGaA in 2004.

197 *Hotdogs with Herb* . . . Baum and Kling, *The Transparent Leader*.

198 *An inspiring tale of remarkable results* . . . Jackie and Kevin Freiberg, *NUTS! Southwest Airlines' Crazy Recipe for Business and Personal Success* (New York: Bard Press, 1996).

199 *Employees are number one* . . . Ibid.

201 *Compliant people simply go through the motions* . . . Ibid.

Chapter 12

206 *When companies engage in small decencies* . . . Interview with Theresa M. Welbourne, Detroit, Michigan, June 2006.

207 *In tough times* . . . Don Manvel et al., "The Nice Guy," *Harvard Business Review*, October 2006, 30.

Index

About the Author

Steve Harrison is chairman of Lee Hecht Harrison, the global performance leader in career management and leadership consulting, and former chief ethics and compliance officer of Adecco Group, the largest human resources solutions company in the world.